# The Hedge
# Fund Mirage

# The Hedge Fund Mirage

*The Illusion of Big Money and Why It's Too Good to Be True*

Simon Lack

**WILEY**

John Wiley & Sons, Inc.

Published by John Wiley & Sons, Inc., Hoboken, New Jersey.

Published simultaneously in Canada.

For general information on our other products and services or for technical support, please contact our Customer Care Department within the United States at (800) 762-2974, outside the United States at (317) 572-3993, or fax (317) 572-4002.

Wiley also publishes its books in a variety of electronic formats. Some content that appears in print may not be available in electronic books. For more information about Wiley products, visit our web site at www.wiley.com.

*Library of Congress Cataloging-in-Publication Data:*
Lack, Simon, 1962-
    The hedge fund mirage : the illusion of big money and why it's too good to be true / Simon Lack. – 1
        p. cm.
    Includes bibliographical references and index.
    ISBN 978-1-118-16431-0 (hardback); ISBN 978-1-118-20618-8 (ebk);
    ISBN 978-1-118-20619-5 (ebk); ISBN 978-1-118-20620-1 (ebk)
  1. Hedge funds.   2. Investments.   I. Title.
    HG4530.L23 2012
    332.64'524–dc23
                                                                2011035473

Printed in the United States of America

10  9  8  7  6  5  4  3  2

*This book is dedicated to my wife Karen and our three wonderful children Jaclyn, Daniel, and Alexandra.*

# Contents

# Introduction

## *Why I Wrote This Book*

I t was early 2008, and I was sitting in a presentation by Blue Mountain, a large and successful hedge fund focused on credit derivatives. Its founder, Andrew Feldstein, had previously worked at JPMorgan, and was widely respected in the industry. JPMorgan had been a pioneer in the development of the market for credit derivatives, instruments which allowed credit risk to be managed independently of the loans or bonds from which they were derived. This was prior to the 2008 credit crisis later that year in which derivatives played a key role, and Blue Mountain had generated reasonable returns based on their deep understanding of this new market. The meeting took place around a large boardroom table with a dozen or more interested investors, and the head of investor relations went through his well-honed explanation of their unique strategy and its superior record.

It was boring, and as my attention drifted away from the speaker, I began flipping through the presentation. Interestingly, Blue Mountain included not just their returns but their annual assets under management (AUM) as well. You could see how their business had grown steadily off the back of solid but unspectacular results. Clearly, everyone involved was enjoying quiet, steady success. I was curious how much profit the investors had actually made, since their returns had been moderating somewhat while AUM continued to grow. I started to scribble down a few numbers and do some quick math. Since Blue Mountain also disclosed their fees, which included both a management fee (a percentage of AUM) and an incentive fee (a share of the investors' profits) there was enough information to estimate how much money the founding partners of Blue Mountain, including its owner Andrew Feldstein, had earned. With what turned out to be good timing in late 2007 they had recently sold a minority stake in their management company to Affiliated Managers Group (AMG), an acquirer of asset management companies. I made a few more calculations. Feldstein was not only very smart, but highly commercial. My back-of-the-envelope calculations showed that the fees earned by Blue Mountain's principals, including the proceeds from its sale to AMG, were roughly equal to all of the profits their investors had made (that is, profits in excess of treasury bills, the riskless alternative). Blue Mountain had made successful bets with other people's money and split the profits 50/50. Was this really why some of the largest institutional investors had been plowing enormous sums of money into the hedge fund industry? Was this a fair split of the profits? Was it even typical of the industry, or were Blue Mountain's principals unusually gifted not only at trading credit derivatives but at retaining an inordinately large share of the gains for themselves? The hedge fund industry had enjoyed many years of phenomenal success, and the collective decisions of thousands of investors, consultants, analysts, and advisors strongly suggested that there must be more value creation going on than my quick calculations implied. So I started to look more closely, and I found that while the hedge fund industry has created some fabulous wealth, most investors have shared in this to a surprisingly modest extent. I tried to think of anyone who had become rich by being a hedge fund investor (other than the managers of hedge fund themselves) and I couldn't.

Many of the professionals advising investors on their hedge fund investments will be familiar with the conceptual disadvantages their clients face as presented in this book. They will likely be surprised at the numbers and may disagree with some of them (though there can be little doubt about the overall result). But the people best situated to tell this story, the people with the necessary knowledge and insight, are busy still making a living from the hedge fund industry and have neither the time nor inclination to stop doing that. I am a product of the hedge fund industry myself, and it has provided me financial security if not membership on the Forbes 500 List. To counter the obvious charge of hypocrisy that readers may level at this industry insider now disdainfully commenting on his profession, please note: My journey through hedge funds was guided by the same principles I espouse but that too few investors follow. Invest off the beaten track, with small undiscovered managers; negotiate preferential terms, including a share of the business or at least preferential fees and reasonable liquidity; demand (and do not accept less) complete transparency about where your money is. If more investors had done so, their investment results would have turned out to be far more acceptable.

But hedge funds will not disappear, at least certainly not by virtue of this book! There are a great many highly talented managers and that will undoubtedly continue for the foreseeable future. The question for hedge fund investors is how they can more reliably identify the good ones and also keep more of the winnings that are generated using their capital. This book attempts to answer those questions.

# Acknowledgments

Many people provided input, support, and ideas as this project made its way to print. I'd especially like to thank Professor Tony Loviscek of Seton Hall University. Tony's encouragement as well as valuable feedback helped take an essay and turn it into something bigger. David Lieberman read the entire manuscript and provided helpful suggestions. Several people also reviewed individual chapters including Andreas Deutschmann, Miles Doherty, Larry Hirshik, Henry Hoffman, and Andrew Weisman. I am indebted to all of them for their time and interest. I'd like to thank Josh Friedlander of *AR* magazine, both for ensuring my original essay on hedge fund returns was published and also for his introduction to John Wiley and Sons, the publisher. Laura Walsh, Judy Howarth, Tula Batanchiev, Melissa Lopez, and Stacey Smith at John Wiley tolerated my impatience with the ponderous publishing calendar and guided this project to completion. Finally I'd like to thank my mother Jeannie Lucas, whose many years in financial journalism were invaluable as the initial editor and enthusiastic supporter of her son's first book.

# The Hedge
# Fund Mirage

# Chapter 1

# The Truth about Hedge Fund Returns

If all the money that's ever been invested in hedge funds had been put in treasury bills instead, the results would have been twice as good. When you stop for a moment to consider this fact, it's a truly amazing statistic. The hedge fund industry has grown from less than $100 billion in assets under management (AUM) back in the 1990s to more than $1.6 trillion today. Some of the biggest fortunes in history have been made by hedge fund managers. In 2009 David Tepper (formerly of Goldman Sachs) topped the Absolute Return list of top earners with $4 billion, followed by George Soros with $3.3 billion (according to the *New York Times*). The top 25 hedge fund managers collectively earned $25.3 billion in 2009, and just to make it into this elite group required an estimated payout of $350 million. Every year, it seems the top earners in finance are hedge fund managers, racking up sums that dwarf even the CEOs of the Wall Street banks that service them. In fact, astronomical earnings for the top managers have almost become routine. It's Capitalism in action, pay for performance, outsized rewards for extraordinary results. Their investment prowess has driven capital and clients to them; Adam Smith's invisible hand has been at work.

## How to Look at Returns

In any case, haven't hedge funds generated average annual returns of 7 percent or even 8 percent (depending on which index of returns you use) while stocks during the first decade of the twenty-first century were a miserable place to be? Surely all this wealth among hedge fund managers has been created because they've added enormous value to their clients. Capitalism, with its efficient allocation of resources and rewards, has channeled investors' capital to these managers and the rest of the hedge fund industry because it's been a good place to invest. If so much wealth has been created, it must be because so much more wealth has been earned by their clients, hedge fund investors. Can an industry with $1.6 trillion in AUM be wrong? There must be many other examples of increased wealth beyond just the hedge fund managers themselves.

Well, like a lot of things it depends on how you add up the numbers. The hedge fund industry in its present form and size is a relatively new phenomenon. Alfred Winslow Jones is widely credited with founding the first hedge fund in 1949. His insight at the time was to combine short positions in stocks he thought were expensive with long positions in those he liked, to create what is today a long/short equity fund. A.W. Jones was hedging, and he enjoyed considerable success through the 1950s and 1960s (Mallaby, 2010). Hedge funds remained an obscure backwater of finance however, and although the number of hedge funds had increased to between 200 and 500 by 1970, the 1973 to 1974 crash wiped most of them out. Even by 1984, Tremont Partners, a research firm, could only identify 68 hedge funds (Mallaby, 2010). Michael Steinhardt led a new generation of hedge fund managers during the 1970s and 1980s, along with George Soros, Paul Jones, and a few others.

But hedge funds remained a cottage industry, restricted by U.S. securities laws to taking only "qualified" (i.e., wealthy and therefore financially sophisticated) clients. Hedge funds began to enjoy a larger profile during the 1990s, and expanded beyond long/short equity to merger arbitrage, event-driven investing, currencies, and fixed-income relative value. Relative value was the expertise of Long Term Capital Management, the team of PhDs and Nobel Laureates that almost brought down the global financial system when their bets went awry in 1998 (Lowenstein). Rather than signaling the demise of hedge funds however, this turned out to be the threshold of a new era of strong growth. Investors began to pay attention to the uncorrelated and consistently positive returns hedge funds were able to generate. By 1997 the industry's AUM had reached $118 billion[1] and LTCM's disaster barely slowed the industry's growth. Investors concluded that the collapse of John Meriwether's fund was an isolated case, more a result of hubris and enormous bad bets rather than anything systematic. Following the dot.com crash of 2000 to 2002, hedge funds proved their worth and generated solid returns. Institutional investors burned by technology stocks were open to alternative assets as a way to diversify risk, and the subsequent growth in the hedge fund industry kicked into high gear. It is worth noting that the vast majority of the capital invested in hedge funds has been there less than 10 years.

## Digging into the Numbers

To understand hedge fund returns you have to understand how the averages are calculated. To use equity markets as an example, in a broad stock market index such as the Standard & Poor's 500, the prices of all 500 stocks are weighted by the market capitalization of each company, and added up. The S&P 500 is a capitalization weighted index, so an investor who wants to mimic the return of the S&P 500 would hold all the stocks in the same weights that they have in the index. Some other stock market averages are based on a float-adjusted market capitalization (i.e., adjusted for those shares actually available to trade) and

[1] BarclayHedge

the venerable Dow Jones Industrial Average is price-weighted (although few investors allocate capital to a stock based simply on its price, its curious construction hasn't hurt its popularity). In some cases an equally weighted index may better reflect an investor's desire to diversify and not invest more in a company just because it's big. On the other hand, a market cap-weighted index like the S&P 500 reflects the experience of all the investors in the market, since bigger companies command a bigger percentage of the aggregate investor's exposure. The stocks in the index are selected, either by a committee or based on a set of rules, and once chosen those companies stay in the index until they are acquired, go bankrupt, or are otherwise removed (perhaps because they have performed badly and shrunk to where they no longer meet the criteria for inclusion).

Calculating hedge fund returns involves more judgment, and is in some ways as much art as science. First, hedge fund managers can choose whether or not to report their returns. Since hedge funds are not registered with the SEC, and hedge fund managers are largely unregulated, the decision on whether to report monthly returns to any of the well-known reporting services belongs to the hedge fund manager. He can begin providing results when he wants, and can stop when he wants without giving a reason. Hedge fund managers are motivated to report returns when they are good, since the main advantage to a hedge fund in publishing returns is to attract attention from investors and grow their business through increased AUM. Conversely, poor returns won't attract clients, so there's not much point in reporting those, unless you've already started reporting and you expect those returns to improve.

This self-selection bias tends to make the returns of the hedge fund index appear to be higher than they should be (Dichev, 2009). Lots of academic literature exists seeking to calculate how much the returns are inflated by this effect (also known as survivor bias, since just as history is written by the victors, only surviving hedge fund managers can report returns). And there's lots of evidence to suggest that when a hedge fund is suffering through very poor and ultimately fatal performance, those last few terrible months don't get reported (Pool, 2008). There's no other reliable way to obtain the returns of a hedge fund except from the manager of the hedge fund itself, so the index provider has little choice but to exclude the fund from his calculations (although the hapless investors obviously experience the dying hedge fund's last miserable months).

Another attractive feature of hedge funds is that when they are small and new, their performance tends to be higher than it is in later years when they're bigger, less nimble, and more focused on generating steady yet still attractive returns (Boyson, 2008). This is accepted almost as an article of faith among hedge fund investors, and there are very good reasons why it's often true. As with any new business that's going to be successful, the entrepreneur throws himself into the endeavor 24/7 and everything else in his life takes a backseat to generating performance, the "product" on which the entire enterprise will thrive or fail. Small funds are more nimble, making it easier to exploit inefficiencies in stocks, bonds, derivatives, or any chosen market. Entering and exiting positions is usually easier when you're managing a smaller amount of capital since you're less likely to move the market much when you trade and others are less likely to notice or care what you're doing. Success brings with it size in the form of a larger base of AUM and the advantages of being small slowly dissipate. Academic research has been done on the benefits of being small as well (Boyson, 2008).

An interesting corner of the hedge fund world involves seeding hedge funds, in which the investor provides capital and other support (such as marketing, office space, and other kinds of business assistance) to a start-up hedge fund in exchange for some type of equity stake in the managers' business. If the hedge fund is successful, the seed provider's equity stake can generate substantial additional returns. A key element behind this strategy is the recognition that small, new hedge funds outperform their bigger, slower cousins. Almost every hedge fund I ever looked at had done very well in its early years. That is how they came to be big and successful. So there's little doubt that surviving hedge funds have better early performance. Sometimes I would meet a small hedge fund manager with, say $10 to $50 million in AUM. In describing the benefits of investing with him, he'd often assert that his small size made him nimble and able to get in and out of positions that others didn't care about without moving the market. I'd typically ask what he felt his advantage would be if he was successful in growing his business. How nimble would he be at, say, $500 million in AUM when the success he'd enjoyed as a small hedge fund (because he was small) had enabled him to move into the next league of managers. Invariably the manager would maintain that his many other advantages (deep research capability, broad industry knowledge, extensive contacts list) would suffice, but it illustrates one of the many conflicting goals faced by hedge funds and their clients.

Investors want hedge funds to stay small so they can continue to exploit the inefficiencies that have brought the investor to this meeting with the hedge fund manager. And the manager naturally wants to grow his business and get rich, so he strives to convince the investor that he won't miss the advantages of being small if and when he becomes bigger. In fact, while small managers will tell you small is beautiful, large managers will brag about greater access to meet with companies, negotiate better financing terms with prime brokers, hire smart analysts, and invest in infrastructure. There can be truth to both arguments, although it's sometimes amusing to watch a manager shift his message as he morphs from small to bigger. The result of all these challenges with calculating exactly how hedge funds have done is that generally the reported returns have been biased higher than they should be (Jorion, 2010).

## The Investor's View of Returns

The problems I've described are faced by all the indices of reported hedge fund returns. However, in assessing how the industry has done, what seems absolutely clear is that you have to use an index that reflects the experience of the average investor. While individual hedge fund investors may have portfolios of hedge funds that are equally weighted so as to provide better diversification, clearly the investors in aggregate are more heavily invested in the larger funds. Calculating industry returns therefore requires using an asset-weighted index (just as the S&P 500 Index is market-cap weighted). Hedge Fund Research in Chicago publishes dozens of indices representing hedge fund returns. They break down the list by sector, geography, and style. A broadly representative index that is asset-weighted and is designed to reflect the industry as a whole is the HFR Global Hedge Fund Index, which they refer to as

HFRX. Using returns from 1998 to 2010, the index has an annual return of 7.3 percent. Compared with this, the S&P 500 (with dividends reinvested) returned 5.9 percent and Treasury bills returned 3.0 percent. Blue chip corporate bonds (as represented by the Dow Jones Corporate Bond Index) generated 7.2 percent. So hedge funds handily beat equities, easily outperformed cash, and did a little better than high-grade corporate bonds.

What's wrong with this picture? The returns are all based on the simple average return each year. The hedge fund industry routinely calculates returns based on the value of $1 invested at inception. And it's true that, based on the HFRX if you had invested $1 million in 1998 you would have earned 7.3 percent per annum. Hedge funds did best in the early years, when the industry was much smaller. Just as small hedge funds can do better than large ones, a small hedge fund industry has done better than a large one. When you adjust for the size of the hedge fund industry (using AUM figures from Barclay-Hedge) the story is completely different. Rather than generating a return of 7.3 percent, hedge funds have returned only 2.1 percent. There were fewer hedge fund investors in 1998 with far less money invested, but based on the strong results the few earned at that time, many more followed. It's the difference between looking at how the average hedge fund did versus how the average investor did. Knowing that the average hedge fund did well isn't much use if the average investor did poorly.

Here's an example that shows the difference between the two. You can think of it as the difference between taking annual returns and averaging them (known as time-weighted returns) and returns weighted for the amount of money invested at each time (known as asset-weighted returns). If more money is invested, then that year's results affect more people and are more important. This is why hedge funds haven't been that good for the average investor, because the average investor only started investing in hedge funds in the last several years.

Imagine for a moment that you found a promising hedge fund manager and invested $1 million in his fund (see Table 1.1). After the first year he's up 50 percent and your $1 million has grown to $1.5 million. Satisfied with the shrewd decision you made to invest with

**Table 1.1**   The Problem With Adding To Winners

---
**Year 1**

You invest $1 million

HF return is 50%

Your investment is worth $1.5 million

Your profit is $500 thousand

**Year 2**

You invest another $1 million (total investment now $2.5 million)

HF return is −40%

Your investment is worth $1.5 million

Your loss is $1 million

---

him, you invest a further $1 million in his fund bringing your investment to $2.5 million. The manager then stumbles badly and loses 40 percent. Your $2.5 million has dropped to $1.5 million. You've lost 25 percent of your capital. Meanwhile, the hedge fund manager has returned +50 percent followed by −40 percent, for an average annual return of around +5 percent[2].

Now let's take a look at how these results will be portrayed. The hedge fund manager will report an average *annual* return over two years of +5 percent (up 50 percent followed by down 40 percent). Meanwhile, his investor has really lost money, and has an internal rate of return (IRR) of −18 percent. IRR[3] is pretty close to the return weighted by the amount of capital invested. It assigns more weight to the second year's negative performance in this example than the first, because the investor had more money at stake. The hedge fund is showing a positive return, while his investor has lost money. In fact, his marketing materials will likely show a geometric annual return of +5.13 percent, while if his investors had all added to their initial investment in this same way in aggregate they would have all lost money.

[2]The geometric return is 5.13 percent

[3]IRR is the discount rate at which all the cash flows from an investment have a net present value of 0. Describing it as the weighted average return is not precisely correct, but is a reasonable approximation.

So is this performance good? Which measure of performance is a more accurate reflection of the hedge fund manager's skill? Should a year of strong performance with a small number of clients be combined with a year of poor performance with more clients without any adjustment for size? In private equity and real estate, if your clients have lost money your returns would reflect that, since they'd be expressed as an IRR. However, the hedge fund industry reports returns like mutual funds and apparently nobody has seen fit to challenge that. As a result it's perfectly legal, and is industry practice. But since hedge fund managers claim to provide absolute returns, and can turn away money, isn't it more fair to show the whole story? While nobody can claim to make money every year, part of what hedge funds are supposed to be providing is hedged exposure. Unlike mutual funds and other long-only managers, hedge funds can not only hedge but can also choose to be under-invested or even not invested. In fact, arguably that is part of the skill for which investors are paying, a hedge fund manager's ability to protect capital, to generate uncorrelated returns, to generate *absolute returns* (i.e., not negative). Hedge funds are even referred to as absolute return strategies and most managers will claim some insight about whether they should be taking lots of risk or being more defensive.

While our investor in this case clearly had unfortunate timing in adding to his position, the hedge fund manager apparently knew no better. One very shrewd hedge fund investor I used to work with would sometimes ask a manager for the aggregate profit and loss (P&L) on his fund. He might see a series of annual returns such as +50 percent, +10 percent and −6 percent with strong asset growth every year and question whether the lifetime P&L is positive or negative. In other words, how have all the investors done? In the example described in the table above, the P&L would be negative $500,000 (i.e., what our investor lost). It may or may not be relevant information. Few investors ask for it—in my opinion many more should.

While the numbers in this example are exaggerated to illustrate the point, this is exactly what investors in hedge funds have done as a group. Although they've come to believe that strong early performance with small size is a reliable part of most hedge funds' history, they've forgotten to apply that same rule to the industry as a whole. Like many individual hedge funds, the industry did best when it was small.

## How the Hedge Fund Industry Grew

Table 1.2 shows hedge fund performance conventionally, with annual returns from stocks, bonds, and cash alongside for comparison. In the late 1990s when the dot.com bubble was building and then during the subsequent bear market in 2000–02 after it burst, hedge funds truly added value. They protected capital and indeed made money. It was this performance that created the surge of client interest in hedge funds that followed. But the strong relative performance that the industry generated when it was small was not repeated as it grew. Following some fairly mediocre years during the middle part of the decade, the Credit Crisis of 2008 led to a 23 percent loss for the year, with only a partial rebound in 2009 and modest returns in 2010. Hedge funds are represented by the HFRX Index. This is an asset-weighted index, which means that the underlying hedge funds it represents are weighted based on their size. Larger hedge funds impact the results of the index more than small ones. Since we're interested in how investors in

**Table 1.2**   Hedge Fund Industry Growth and Asset Class Returns

| Year | Hedge Fund Industry Assets (Billions) | Hedge Fund Returns (HFRX) | S&P 500 (with dividends reinvested) | Dow Jones Corporate Bonds | Treasury Bills |
|------|------|------|------|------|------|
| 1998 | $   143 | 12.9% | 28.6% | 10.3% | 5.1% |
| 1999 | $   189 | 26.7% | 21.0% | −2.9% | 4.8% |
| 2000 | $   237 | 14.3% | −9.1% | 9.4% | 6.2% |
| 2001 | $   322 | 8.7% | −11.9% | 10.7% | 3.9% |
| 2002 | $   505 | 4.7% | −22.1% | 11.3% | 1.7% |
| 2003 | $   826 | 13.4% | 28.7% | 9.9% | 1.1% |
| 2004 | $1,229 | 2.7% | 10.9% | 6.2% | 1.3% |
| 2005 | $1,361 | 2.7% | 4.9% | 1.3% | 3.2% |
| 2006 | $1,713 | 9.3% | 15.8% | 3.8% | 4.9% |
| 2007 | $2,137 | 4.2% | 5.5% | 5.2% | 4.8% |
| 2008 | $1,458 | −23.3% | −37.0% | 1.8% | 1.7% |
| 2009 | $1,554 | 13.4% | 26.5% | 17.6% | 0.1% |
| 2010 | $1,694 | 5.2% | 15.1% | 8.8% | 0.1% |

AUM data from BarclayHedge; HF Returns from Hedge Fund Research; S&P 500 data from Bloomberg; Corp Bonds from Dow Jones; Treasury Bills from Federal Reserve

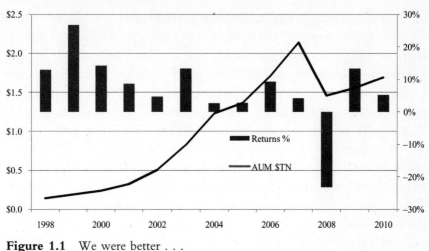

**Figure 1.1**  We were better . . .

aggregate have done, it makes sense to use an asset-weighted index, since large hedge funds figure more prominently both in the index and in investors' results. Figures 1.1 and 1.2 compare hedge fund returns and size of the industry in two ways.

Figure 1.1 presents returns conventionally, so each bar represents the annual return for that year.

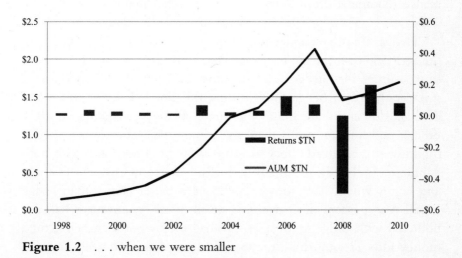

**Figure 1.2**   . . . when we were smaller

Figure 1.2 converts annual returns to profits and losses based on the AUM in the industry at each time. It shows the annual returns in money terms to hedge fund investors each year. In 2010 two academics, Ilia Dichev from Goizueta Business School at Emory University in Atlanta, Georgia, and Gwen Yu from Harvard Business School in Cambridge, Massachusetts, produced a research paper ("Higher Risk, Lower Returns: What Hedge Fund Investors Really Earn") that performed a similar though more detailed analysis of hedge fund returns. Their study went back to 1980 and arrived at the same conclusion, that overall industry returns had been a disappointment for hedge fund investors. This chart illustrates just how catastrophic 2008 was for investors since the losses from that year dwarf previous returns.

The strong returns of the late 1990s were nice for the investors that participated, but there weren't that many of them and their allocations were small. By the time the Credit Crisis hit with full force in 2008 a great many new investors had "discovered" hedge funds without having benefitted from the strong returns of the past. *In fact, in 2008 the hedge fund industry lost more money than all the profits it had generated during the prior 10 years.* Although it's not possible to calculate precisely, it's likely that hedge funds in 2008 lost all the profits ever made. By the end of 2008, the cumulative results of all the hedge fund investing that had gone before were negative. The average investor was down. For hedge fund investors it had been an expensive experiment. Although performance rebounded from 2009 to 2010, it didn't dramatically alter the story.

Hedge funds have indeed done better than stocks. The IRR from the S&P 500 over the last ten years from 2001–2010 is only 1.1 percent (this assumes that hedge fund investors had put all their money in stocks rather than hedge funds during this time). Equities had a bad decade. But corporate bonds did much better, generating an IRR of 6.3 percent—or more than five times what the average hedge fund investor received. Since most investors hold portfolios with both equities and bonds in them, virtually any combination of stocks and bonds would have turned out to be a better choice than hedge funds. And perhaps most damning of all, if all the investors had not bothered with hedge funds at all, but had simply put their hedge fund money into Treasury bills, they would have done better, earning 2.3

percent. And this doesn't include the cost of investing in hedge funds. Deciding which Treasury bill to buy is not a particularly taxing job, but selecting hedge funds requires either a significant investment in a team of hedge fund analysts, risk management, due diligence, and financial experts, or the use of a hedge fund of funds that employs the same expertise. Either way, it costs an additional 0.5 to 1.0 percent annually for an investor to be in hedge funds, whether through fees paid to the hedge fund of funds manager or increased overhead of an investment team.

## The Only Thing That Counts Is Total Profits

Now, we've just calculated that hedge fund investors as a whole have not been particularly well served by their decision to invest in hedge funds, based on weighted-average-capital invested, or IRR. Is this a fair way to calculate results? The hedge fund industry and the consultants that serve it have stayed with the since-inception, value-of-the-first-dollar approach. While there's little doubt that hedge fund investors haven't done well, is that the right way to look at it? 2008 was a terrible year for just about any investment strategy apart from government bonds. Hedge funds weren't the only group to have lost money, and some investors expressed relief as results rolled in during 2008 and into 2009 that their hedge funds hadn't done worse! Investors facing portfolios of equities that had lost more than a third of their value, high-yield bond positions for which no reliable market even existed, and private equity investments that had stopped generating cash from liquidity events might be forgiven for regarding being down 23 percent as an acceptable result.

2008 was in so many ways a thousand-year flood, although amazingly for many investors, already so committed to the inclusion of hedge funds in their portfolios in spite of the evidence to the contrary, it represented acceptable performance. Most of the hedge fund industry, including the managers themselves, the investors, the consultants that advise them, the prime brokers, and private banks are all heavily invested in the continued success of the industry. I'll simply note that hedge funds became popular as absolute return vehicles, meaning that they were expected to make money (i.e., an absolute return, not one with a negative sign in front of it) and were uncorrelated with other markets. In 2008 they failed on both counts, but it turns out hedge fund investors are a fairly forgiving lot and while there were some modest pro-investor changes that followed, the investors generally stuck with it.

But what about the use of IRR, or dollar-weighted returns, to assess how the hedge fund industry has done. Is this a fair way to analyze it or not? In general, if an investment manager doesn't have much control over asset flows in and out of the strategy, it's reasonable to calculate returns based on the value-of-the-first-dollar method. This is commonly the case with mutual funds. Since money flows into and out of mutual funds based on investors' appetite, it seems fair enough to judge a mutual fund manager based on the first dollar. He generally can't control whether his sector is in favor or not, and the vast majority of mutual funds are long-only, meaning they're not hedged. Market movements will typically determine most of a mutual fund's returns, and that's beyond the control of a mutual fund manager. On the other hand, private equity and real estate funds are routinely evaluated based on IRR. This also seems fair, since the typical structure requires a commitment of capital to the fund with the investment manager deciding when to call that capital over time. Since the commitments are usually quite long term, three to 10 years, and the manager of the fund decides when he wants the money (presumably when an attractive investment opportunity is available) it seems fair to judge him on total dollars invested, since he controls the timing.

## Hedge Funds Are Not Mutual Funds

So should hedge funds be judged like mutual funds, based on the first dollar invested? Or like private equity, based on total dollars? Hedge fund managers always have the option to turn away investors. The industry has largely marketed itself as focused on absolute returns, but within each strategy there are good and bad times to be invested. Indeed, many of the largest hedge fund managers have in the past closed to new capital, either because they felt the opportunities they were seeing weren't that great or because they felt that adding to their AUM would reduce their investing flexibility and dilute returns.

Often in such cases the hedge fund manager is himself the biggest single investor in the fund, so his desire to avoid diluting returns is not only good for his current investors but of course good for his own investment too. In other cases a hedge fund will announce some limited capacity available to current investors before closing. Rather like jumping on the train before it leaves the station, this can often draw in additional assets from investors who fear being unable to add to their investment later on. The point is that hedge fund managers are much more like private equity managers in that they can control whether to accept additional money into their fund or not. The bigger, more established funds generally have more clout in this regard than smaller funds, and of course the bigger managers are by definition more prominently figured in an asset-weighted index like the HFRX.

The hedge fund industry has grown on the basis of generating uncorrelated, absolute returns and having insight into when to deploy capital into and out of different strategies, sectors, and opportunities. If every hedge fund investor asked each hedge fund manager prior to investing whether this is a good time to be investing, the responses would vary but would rarely be no. But hedge fund managers have routinely turned away investors and even returned capital if they felt it was in their investors' interests or their interests, or both. Sometimes that was to the investors' subsequent benefit. In 1997 Long Term Capital Management decided to return some capital to their investors (Lowenstein). They had earned so much in fees that were reinvested back in their own fund that the clients' capital was making them too big and diluting returns. This illustrates another negative optionality hedge fund investors face; if you select a hedge fund manager that is wildly successful, you'll wind up paying him so much in fees that he'll no longer want or need to manage your money. Successful hedge fund investing can be its own worst enemy! However, fortunately for the investors in LTCM, the return of capital, while unpopular at the time, saved many of them from greater losses when the fund eventually destroyed itself with leveraged bets gone bad in 1998.

In general, individual hedge fund managers have exercised much greater control over their size than many mutual funds; the hedge fund industry is much closer to private equity in this regard, and therefore assessing results in the same way as private equity seems to make sense. And on that basis, while the hedge fund industry has generated fabulous wealth and created many fortunes, it has largely done so for itself. To use that oft-repeated Wall Street saying, where are the customers' yachts? Most of us can probably name a few billionaire hedge fund managers, but who can name even one hedge fund investor whose fortune is based on the hedge funds he successfully picked? David Swensen, who manages Yale University's endowment and led its shift into hedge funds in the 1990s, grew Yale's endowment substantially through this early move. By 2005 his investment picks were credited with having generated $7.8 billion of Yale's $15 billion endowment (Mallaby, 2010).

No doubt David Swensen is a very talented investor, and Yale had the foresight to invest in hedge funds earlier than most other institutions. But $7.8 billion is around 3 percent of all the profits investors earned from hedge funds since 1998 (and given the industry's small size prior to this, probably in their entire history). Yale's hedge fund portfolio at its peak was probably around $10 billion, less than 1 percent of the industry. If Yale has earned a bigger share of the hedge fund industry's profits than the size of their portfolio deserves, then others must have done worse. Clearly, few other hedge fund investors have done as well as Yale.

## Summary

Hedge fund investors in aggregate have not done nearly as well as popularly believed. The media focus on the profits of the top managers has obscured the absence of wealthy clients. Although the industry performed well in the 1990s, it was small and there weren't many investors. In recent years as its rapid growth has continued, results have suffered and many more investors have lived through mediocre returns compared with those enterprising few that found hedge funds when the industry itself was undiscovered. The control that managers have over when to take clients as well as the reliable drop in returns that occurs with increased size mean that assessing aggregate returns across all investors is a fair way to assess the results. Now let's take a look back at what it was like investing in hedge funds 15 or more years ago, when Peter Lynch was still the best known money manager having retired from running the Magellan mutual fund at Fidelity in 1990, and only an elite cognoscenti even knew where to find a hedge fund manager.

# Chapter 2

# The Golden Age of Hedge Funds

My own direct involvement with hedge funds began in 1994. Following yet another bank merger (this one between Manufacturers Hanover Trust and Chemical Bank in 1992) we had been combining trading units with the typical merger directive of exploiting revenue synergies (i.e., ensure $2 + 2 = 5$) while cutting costs. In 1996 we merged with Chase Manhattan Bank, so now three large New York money center banks (Manufacturers Hanover Trust, Chemical Bank, and Chase) had been combined into one. In 2000 Chase and JPMorgan merged creating a colossus that was so big it retained both names (Chase for retail banking and JPMorgan for institutional business). To keep it simple I'll use the name in existence at each point, since the timing of each merger isn't relevant to the story.

## Hedge Funds as Clients

David Puth was a highly respected manager of the foreign exchange (FX) business and he retained that role through successive combinations. David was a very driven executive who combined a deep interest in financial markets with a strong focus on key client relationships. He possessed an entrepreneurial business sense and every day was filled with relentless frantic activity. Discussions were often brief and left unfinished as David rushed from one client call or markets meeting to the next. He was extremely effective and was able to consistently grow his division's revenues and profits every year in spite of the fact that FX was already a highly developed and competitive business. Every day David burst into the office at 7 a.m. or earlier completely energized for the day ahead, having already worked out at home upon waking. He was hard-driving and demanded 110 percent dedication and effort from his management team, but he led by example and certainly gave no less himself. Under David's leadership the FX business had built a strong following amongst many of the biggest hedge funds at a time when global macro was the dominant investing style.

As a result of a reorganization of the trading division, my interest rate business was moved into David's expanding orbit. One of David's qualities was that he was always thinking of new revenue opportunities— he behaved more as a business owner than an employee. Chase was already transacting large volumes of FX with many of the biggest hedge funds, who valued the ready liquidity Chase could provide. David realized that this offered a unique perspective on the trading styles of many hedge fund managers, and perhaps could provide insight into which managers were most profitable in their FX trading activities. Something as simple as observing how a market might move following a large hedge fund trade could reveal managers with skill and foresight compared to those who tended to have poor timing. The traders at Chase who took the other side of the hedge fund trades would know that some transactions needed to be hedged out immediately to avoid a loss, while others might allow more time for the risk to be offset. David set up a business referred to as the Outside Advisors Program, whose objective was to invest in those hedge fund clients that demonstrated the most insight at trading FX. Since Chase was frequently on the opposite side of the trades these managers did, we could see which ones were good at calling the next move in currencies and which weren't. Knowing which ones were generally profitable would be helpful in deciding where to invest.

Shakil Riaz managed the Outside Advisors Program for David. Shakil is something of a legend in the hedge fund industry. Originally from Pakistan, he had run Chemical Bank's Bahrain office before moving to New York. In the years since he began investing in hedge funds he has become widely known throughout the industry through his regular attendance at the many conferences held around the world at which hedge fund professionals congregate. If someone in the industry knew only one person at JPMorgan, it was likely to be Shakil. Over the years he built an enviable track record in an old-fashioned and somewhat unconventional way. His investment team was simply Shakil and his research analyst Anthony Marzigliano, and Shakil's judgment and network of contacts were the primary tools he used to identify and select hedge fund managers. Shakil turned out to be a shrewd judge of character, and developed an uncanny ability to ferret out talented managers early in their careers while their returns were strong, AUM relatively small, and before others had found them. Even more importantly, he was adept at avoiding the ones that turned out to disappoint or to be frauds. He showed almost a sixth sense for danger—an inconsistent answer to a benign question or a questionable reference could be enough to give him pause and avoid an investment that he might otherwise later regret. Shakil's hard-nosed assessment of managers is neatly covered by an engaging personality. He's unfailingly good company and it's impossible not to have a good time with him. He has many entertaining stories about people he's met over the years, and invariably those who have dealt with him found it a positive experience. On more than one occasion I've met hedge fund managers that I knew Shakil had rejected, who talk about him as if old friends. Shakil is one of the nicest people I know and a man of true integrity.

At the time I was getting to know David Puth, Shakil had been managing the nascent hedge fund business for a couple of years. It turns out that in the FX business there are often just a handful of good trading opportunities in a year (after all, there are far fewer individual currencies to trade than stocks or bonds). Sometimes the best FX traders weren't even primarily focused on FX. They might believe that the U.S. dollar would depreciate over the next several months, put the trade on and forget about it, adjusting their position only rarely. Meanwhile, traders who were FX specialists often felt compelled to trade more frequently, and as a result could incur losses on other less-compelling ideas that would subtract from their overall returns. The early results of the program were therefore mixed, but to David's and Shakil's credit they weren't discouraged. They concluded that what was needed was a more diversified portfolio to include hedge funds pursuing convertible bond arbitrage, equity pairs trading, and fixed-income relative value. The Capital Markets Investment Program (CMIP) was born. I often marveled at David's willingness and ability to grow a hedge fund investing portfolio out of an FX trading business. We knew of no other bank that had tried anything similar, although in subsequent years others did follow, as the success of the CMIP program grew. While it would have been a logical move to have CMIP consider investments in some of the bigger clients, Shakil always adamantly refused to allow his process to be distorted by anything other than an appraisal of the investment merits of each manager. Whenever an FX salesman would petition Shakil to invest with a new hedge fund in order to generate additional FX business, Shakil would ask if the salesman would contribute his sales credits to cover any potential investment losses. Nobody ever took him up on it.

## Building a Hedge Fund Portfolio

I joined the CMIP investment committee, which also included David's highly likeable and hard-working business manager Bob Flicker. As the portfolio was growing, David wanted someone with a trading background involved in the investment process. Typically Shakil would schedule a meeting with a manager that he liked. We'd all meet with him in a conference room and take turns asking questions as we attempted to understand how he made money, what drove his returns, how much he might lose, and generally form an opinion as to whether this manager's fund belonged in our portfolio. Although we obviously examined returns and periods of underperformance, the process itself was essentially qualitative. We were interviewing the manager rather as we might interview a trader to join the FX business. Shakil eschewed statistical tools such as mean variance optimization and other techniques that treat hedge funds like stocks and use elements of the Capital Asset Pricing Model (CAPM) to construct an "efficient" portfolio. Instead, his network of contacts in the industry, combined with his own judgment, resulted in a diverse stable of strong managers and one of the most consistent track records of anyone in the industry.

In the 1990s, the hedge fund industry was just beginning to emerge from its past as primarily a high-net-worth, private-bank-client preserve. Hedge funds generally maintained a low profile, and often some of the best managers were identified through referrals rather than through any formal search. Sometimes Shakil would bring in an unknown manager that a friend had mentioned to him, and, in the ensuing few years, strong performance would attract far greater attention. The hedge fund managers themselves were also quite accessible. Frequently we'd visit a manager at his office and would meet in conference rooms more like a client meeting room of a large private bank, with fine leather upholstered chairs, cherry wood tables, and books lining the walls. It felt a little like visiting somebody's Park Avenue home and sitting in their personal library, and added to the overall feeling of exclusivity.

We met with Marc Lasry, who runs Avenue Capital Management, once in just such a setting. Avenue invests in distressed debt, and was founded by Marc and his sister, Sonja. Marc is utterly charming, and we had a most enjoyable and wide-ranging discussion about broad investing themes, the state of the world, and business philosophy. It was all so pleasant, and combined with Marc's silky smooth manner it didn't feel at all like work. We were spending an hour or two in very comfortable surroundings discussing big issues. Asking difficult questions would have seemed totally incongruous, rather like raising an embarrassing family issue at a dinner party. When we asked if we could see the portfolio on a regular basis, Marc said we were welcome to stop by any time and he'd talk about any position we liked. This was portfolio transparency at that time—there would be no computer file e-mailed every month with a list of positions, or access granted to the fund's custodian, but instead we could visit anytime we were in the neighborhood and chat. Avenue of course continued to be very successful, and behind Marc Lasry's warm, engaging personality is a very sound investment process.

## The Interview *Is* the Investment Research

Israel "Izzy" Englander is one of the most colorful characters in the hedge fund industry. Izzy runs his hedge fund as a collection of traders in often unrelated strategies. He sits at the top, allocating capital, monitoring risk, and hiring and firing, but doesn't typically manage large chunks of the firm's capital. Izzy is a tough, street-smart New Yorker who's cynical and has the paranoia of many successful managers that somebody knows more than he does about a trading position he might have and that it's going to cost him money. With his thinning white hair and slight physique he doesn't stand out in a crowd, but Izzy is a survivor and a hugely successful one at that. At times he's probably sailed too close to the edge of what's permissible—the mutual fund timing issue that embroiled his fund Millennium resulted in a $180 million settlement with the Securities and Exchange Commission (SEC) in 2005.

Meanwhile, meetings with Izzy were some of the most entertaining we had with any manager. Using a combination of colloquialisms and his tough Jewish New Yorker persona, Izzy would regale us with tales of trades and traders gone bad, all of which served to highlight his obsessively close oversight of the trading as well as entertain his audience. One of his traders became entangled in a bad position and ". . . got his tits twisted". Another, following an extended period of success was trading larger and larger positions until "The God of Size" paid him a visit, with commensurate financial losses that swiftly ended his career with Millenium. Recounting conversations Izzy had with various traders in his employ, it was clear he translated every loss into his own personal share based on his large investment in the fund. "That guy cost me $2 million before I shut him down," would be a typical assessment of a trader gone bad. Izzy would sit in the meeting room and simply ask what we wanted to know. The conversation would move briskly through episodes of trades that had worked and those that hadn't, interspersed with Izzy's own views about opportunities, all spliced together with humor but also illustrating his tight control over the business. In many ways Izzy is a uniquely colorful personality and represents what makes hedge fund due diligence so interesting.

Occasionally the "CMIP Brain Trust" (as Shakil jokingly referred to his colleagues on the investment committee) would travel together to visit a number of managers. One such trip took place in 1999 to San Francisco during the latter stages of the tech bubble. Many hedge funds located in the Bay area unsurprisingly invested in technology stocks, and Shakil scheduled an entire day of meetings with similarly focused managers. As we moved from one meeting to another within the compact area that is San Francisco's financial district, we heard several managers discuss positions in the same stock. The Internet was white hot, fortunes were being made almost overnight, and hedge funds were constantly searching for the next new thing. Sanchez Computer was a name that came up in every meeting we had, as a stock with enormous potential in using the Internet to streamline some of the services provided by banks. As the day drew to a close we went to our last meeting, which was with a hedge fund specializing in short selling.

Very few hedge fund managers choose to run short-biased or fully short portfolios. As they'll freely admit, it is incredibly difficult to do well. You are fighting against the natural trend of the market to rise over time, and you're also fighting against management and, of course, all the stakeholders who go to work every day intending to drive the stock price higher and force you out of your position at a loss. And then there's the highly unattractive risk profile, the complete inverse of a long position, in that the short has limited potential profit (the stock can't go any lower than 0) and theoretically unlimited upside. As a result, short sellers tend to be an extremely thick-skinned breed with strong opinions invariably supported by very high-quality research.

In fact, some of the most thorough research of stocks is done by short sellers—they have to be thorough because the consequences of a mistake can be so expensive. In many cases, the short seller doesn't just believe the stock is overpriced, but thinks it may be a fraud. Their research has led them to expect the senior management to leave the company one day in handcuffs. Whereas a traditional equity-oriented hedge fund manager can like the company but not always like the stock (depending on its valuation), a short seller always believes the stock is too high, and a worthwhile sale at almost any price. So shorting stocks has never been easy—and shorting tech stocks in the late 1990s might well have been not merely reckless but impossible to do safely. Nonetheless, Shakil had managed to identify one such fund, by way of providing a contrasting view of the world, and we duly showed up to meet them late in the afternoon.

We walked into an office that certainly lacked the appearance of a thriving business. There was no receptionist (she had been laid off) and partially filled cardboard boxes were sitting about. It was eerily quiet. We met the manager, and filed into a conference room. The tone of the conversation was one you'd use in discussing a recently deceased relative. Shakil took on a very sympathetic demeanor, as we all nodded gravely at the irrationality of the market, and Internet stocks in particular. We listened as the manager reviewed the astronomical earnings multiples of many favored names, and agreed that it would surely all end very badly.

Finally we moved on to some more specific positions that this manager had taken, by way of illustrating his style and the quality of his analysis. Since the mood of the office as well as the investment results before us revealed that losing trades had clearly outnumbered winning ones, we asked about some of the more significant losers and what the manager had learnt from those experiences. Sure enough, he brought up Sanchez Computer as an example of a position that had gone against him. We'd heard just about every previous manager during the day discussing a long position in Sanchez, so we were familiar with the bullish case and interested to hear the opposite view. Sanchez was, in this poor guy's view, highly overpriced and generating barely any profit.

The manager recounted how he'd established a short position, and then listened in growing horror one morning as the news on the radio announced that Sanchez Computer had reached an agreement to build Wells Fargo's web site. Knowing this would be (presumably yet another) very bad day, he arrived at work and determined that he'd need to buy back half the short position. He explained that he'd shorted the stock at $20, bought back half the position at $40, and that it was now trading at $50. Although that meant it had more than doubled from where he first sold it, many popular stocks had increased by multiples, and in the spirit of providing moral support and sympathy we noted that things could have been much worse. "No," he replied, "the stock split two for one."

So in fact the stock had increased fivefold from his initial entry point, no doubt consuming substantially too much of his fast-disappearing capital and contributing to the solemn and funereal atmosphere in which we found ourselves. With admirable self control, we concluded the meeting, while stifling our helpless laughter until we were safely out of the building. We wished the poor man better luck in the future. Shortly afterward his hedge fund closed. Sanchez Computer never traded much higher, and in 2004 was acquired by Fidelity National for only $6.17, a 40 percent premium to its price at the time.

## Long Term Capital Management

The 1998 collapse of Long Term Capital Management (LTCM), the Nobel-laureate-run hedge fund founded by John Meriwether, represented a watershed for the industry. Never before had a hedge fund's demise threatened the very stability of the financial system, such that the Federal Reserve felt compelled to organize a bailout of the fund by the Wall Street banks that traded with it. Roger Lowenstein wrote the definitive story in "When Genius Failed," a highly readable record of events. While our hedge fund portfolio did suffer a loss on its investment, prior returned capital ensured an acceptable return. Meanwhile, LTCM was a highly profitable client of Chase's derivatives trading business, both in London and New York.

As a key client, there were regular contacts amongst senior members of the fund and Chase. When LTCM was close to the peak of its influence, it approached Chase with a proposition. Capacity to invest in the best hedge funds has always been highly sought after. LTCM had been so successful that the partners' fees earned on their clients' invested capital had grown to such a degree that they had less need of client capital to run their fund. In fact, since even LTCM was reaching liquidity limits in its chosen markets, having clients was starting to become a bit of an inconvenience, in that it was diluting the returns the partners were able to earn on their own money. As a result, they had been steadily returning capital to investors, upsetting many clients in the process. They were also "closed" to new investors unless there was some "strategic" benefit such as a foreign central bank that might provide market insight helpful to their strategies. Several foreign governmental agencies invested, including the Government of Singapore Investment Corporation, the Bank of Taiwan, and the Kuwaiti state-run pension fund. Italy's central bank invested $100 million through its foreign exchange office (Lowenstein). The best hedge fund managers are not only highly talented market practitioners, but also keenly aware of commercial opportunities when they see them. The partners of LTCM were no exception, and they came up with a structure that would allow investors some scarce capacity in their fund as well as partially relieve the tax burden that success was creating.

Since the founders of LTCM included Myron Scholes, as in the Black-Scholes option pricing algorithm widely used on Wall Street, they had more than a passing familiarity with option theory. They approached a number of banks, including Chase, and offered us the "opportunity" to buy a put option on the future performance of LTCM. If the fund did poorly, the option would increase in value to the buyer, and if the fund did well it would, of course, lose value. Although this option was highly customized and not like the conventional interest rate and FX options we were trading, it was clear that the option buyer would need to hedge the put option by going "long" LTCM, or investing in the fund.

Because betting on poor performance by LTCM was hardly going to be a desirable position, it was highly likely that any buyer would want to "delta hedge" the option with such an investment. Given that LTCM was not accepting new investors, except in certain circumstances, this was a way for an investor to acquire additional investment capacity if they could agree on a premium to pay for the put option. And almost certainly the partners of LTCM, while recognizing that the put option they were selling had some theoretical value, probably believed that over time it would expire worthless, as their low-risk relative-value trading continued to generate profits.

At the time, I was running interest rate derivatives trading, which included options book in all kinds of interest rate options, as well as sitting on the investment committee that oversaw our investment in LTCM's hedge fund. The fund had approached its most senior contacts at Chase to offer us the "opportunity" to participate in this trade. I was asked to evaluate it. An important element of success in trading is a healthy amount of paranoia; while sometimes misplaced, it will often keep you out of trouble. You need to know what you don't know. Options trading involves the use of mathematical models that are only as good as the inputs.

The most generic equity options model requires knowing the strike price on the option, time to expiration, volatility of the underlying stock, and a few other things as well in order to produce an estimated value for the option. In addition, there are assumptions about how stocks move (whether their returns are lognormally distributed, which means roughly they look like a classic bell curve) and also that you can buy and sell the underlying stock (which in this case was going to be an investment in LTCM's fund) at any time. None of these assumptions was valid in the case of this unusual put option. Estimating the volatility of their returns was subject to all kinds of uncertainty, and in fact nothing about the option lent itself to any kind of traditional evaluation.

LTCM was a very large client, not only for Chase but for every bank on Wall Street. The large volumes they trade, the consistently profitable results, and the star power of John Meriwether and his partners meant it was courted by the most-senior executives of every major bank. Chase was no exception, and a member of the bank's executive committee was assigned to manage this "key relationship." Although there was clearly a strong appetite to at least show a price on the trade, I felt it was too far from our expertise to price comfortably. I passed this opinion back up the chain of command. Within a couple of days, the message came back helpfully that, "If you're having trouble pricing this trade, Myron would be happy to stop by and discuss it." Myron as in Scholes, as in Black-Scholes. Much as it would have been fascinating to meet him, since I spent part of every day dealing with the consequences of his insight, I declined. Trading options with Myron Scholes didn't sound like a poker game I should join.

We passed, and as Roger Lowenstein recounts delightfully in his abovementioned book, UBS Capital Markets Group "won" the trade, immediately selling it at a profit internally to their less price-sensitive colleagues in UBS Treasury. Winning the trade allowed UBS to hedge their option by making a substantial direct investment in LTCM's fund, something heavily sought by many investors. It turned out to be a unique version of the Winner's Curse, and as a result UBS ultimately lost $700 million when LTCM collapsed (Lowenstein), taking the additional capacity UBS had been awarded with them.

David Pflug was Chase's head of Credit at the time. David was a patrician banker of the old school, a true gentleman who, though he appeared in manner from another age, was very comfortable overseeing the growth of credit risk through derivatives and other more exotic instruments. He was heavily involved in the bail-out of LTCM and is widely credited with protecting Chase, as well as acting in the best interests of the financial system overall. When Roger Lowenstein had finished his book on LTCM, I bought several copies as gifts and asked him to sign them for the recipients. Roger had interviewed David Pflug for his book, and his inscription to David said, "There are many banks but few bankers. Here's to someone who epitomizes the term." I thought it was a most fitting description. "Greeks" is the shorthand expression for the mathematical derivatives used in managing options risk (delta, gamma, theta, and so on) and such terms were undoubtedly part of everyday conversation at LTCM with their enormous derivatives portfolios. David once commented of John Meriwether and his partners, ". . . for all their knowledge of Greek, they didn't understand the meaning of the word hubris[1]"—an accurate diagnosis.

## Too Many Bank Mergers

Hedge funds weren't the only ones in the go-go late 1990s that were growing strongly and over reaching in their search for bigger and newer sources of profits. Banks were too, and, for as long as anyone can remember, mergers and acquisitions have been a familiar part of the landscape, as larger money center banks gobbled up smaller ones to achieve "scale" or add pieces that were "missing from their full service

[1]The point being that hubris is derived from the Greek word *hybris*.

platform." My career took me from Manufacturers Hanover Trust to Chemical Bank followed by Chase Manhattan and JPMorgan without ever having to resign, as one big combination succeeded another, with smaller acquisitions taking place along the way. Part of the justification for building banking organizations with global reach was to better respond to the needs of their clients. Hedge funds were going global during this time, expanding in Asia and in emerging markets. It would overstate the case to say hedge funds were a primary factor in the serial mergers that culminated with JPMorgan Chase, but servicing them in every major financial market was certainly a fast-growing source of profits for investment banks.

In my experience, bank mergers are grossly over rated, especially from the viewpoint of the acquiring bank. The CEO of the combined entity has job security, since his role was agreed as part of the merger, but everybody else faces uncertainty over their own position, the additional work of merger integration, and the ongoing need to carry out their current responsibilities. On top of that, the acquiring bank's shareholders suffer dilution while the acquired entity receives a takeover premium, as well as immediate vesting of any restricted stock they own through the triggering of "change of control" rules. We went through so many mergers through the 1980s and 1990s that you could anticipate the Orwellian communication from the CEO: This combination is transformational, it will create a full-service platform, we'll be the leading financial services company, and so on.

Bill Harrison was occasionally guilty of poor timing. He perhaps had the misfortune to be running Chase during the late 1990s when markets were buoyant and approaching the 2000 climax of the Internet bubble. However, he made some breathtakingly destructive acquisitions in his quest to build a larger organization. In September 1999 Chase acquired San Francisco-based Hambrecht and Quist for $1.35 billion. H&Q, as they were known, had been busy bringing all kinds of Internet start-ups to market through initial public offerings (IPOs), and buying them looked like a simple way to increase Chase's banking exposure to that fast growing sector. In an indication that Chase's appetite for acquisitions wasn't yet sated, Vice Chairman Marc Shapiro described it as, ". . . an investment in the new economy . . ." but added that it was not, ". . . the total solution to the global platform we are looking for . . ." Stockholders had been warned. By the time the transaction closed Chase enjoyed one full quarter of technology-related investment banking fees in early 2000, before equity markets peaked and the Internet bubble slowly burst. H&Q's CEO Dan Case had sold out at the high, something his brother Steve would achieve with spectacular success at around the same time, when he sold AOL to Time Warner. The Case brothers knew how to sell high.

With money still left to spend, in 2000 Chase acquired Robert Fleming, a very old British bank with far-flung operations across Asia and other developing countries. On paper it looked like a good strategic fit, since at that time Chase was still lacking scale in its Asian operations. Fleming was run as a disparate collection of locally owned and managed businesses, with myriad special deals and ownership stakes by various senior executives. It might have been a good business, but the price paid bore no relation to the value of the business. Chase paid £4.9 billion ($7.8 billion), an amount that the *Economist* reported at the time was far higher than expected and 40 percent more than Commerzbank had offered a year earlier. In an illustration of just how badly Bill Harrison negotiated, it turned out that the amortization of the goodwill on the acquisition was more than the revenues. Chase had accounted for the excess over book value that they paid for Fleming by creating an asset called goodwill, which, under the accounting standards at the time, had to be depreciated. The deal was so overpriced that even the daily revenues of the Fleming businesses couldn't offset the drag on Chase's income statement from this depreciation. Many executives from Fleming took the money and ran, unable to believe their luck at being bought out on such generous terms. Strategic acquisitions can justify just about any price, and Bill Harrison always commented that he spent a great deal of time considering business strategy and possible combinations. Sometimes his focus on the long term trumped short-term considerations of price.

Chase followed the Fleming deal up in May 2000 with a relatively minor acquisition of the Beacon Group for $450 to $500 million. Beacon Group was a small investment advisory firm run by Geoff Boisi and some colleagues from Goldman Sachs, and had about 120 employees, so the company was valued at a startling $4 million per employee. This transaction wasn't really about acquiring a good business at all, but was Bill's answer to succession management in that Geoff Boisi was now in line to run Chase following Bill's retirement. In that regard it failed dismally, since Boisi mishandled his new role as head of Chase's investment bank and was unceremoniously forced out two years later. $500 million, plus presumably a generous severance agreement, had been spent on behalf of Chase's long-suffering shareholders.

To be fair though, Bill Harrison's last deal (following the huge 2000 merger with JPMorgan) was the combination with Banc One in 2004 that shortly thereafter led to Jamie Dimon running the company. If a CEO's most important job is identifying his successor, Bill Harrison's final transaction was an unqualified success.

## Summary

In its early days a small number of intrepid investors accepted that hedge funds were unregulated, pursued obscure trading strategies, and were run in private by highly talented yet largely unkown traders. Investors traded tips on new managers they'd discovered and who was doing well. Making such investments out of a bank's FX trading business represented just the type of unconventional thinking that was a hallmark of the first movers. The due diligence was almost totally qualitative, with personal judgment the critical factor. Although LTCM precipitated a financial crisis, the industry quickly rebounded and scaled new heights. As it grew, different specializations developed and the stunning personal fortunes earned by the top managers caused some investors to look for opportunities to partner early with tomorrow's stars. Hedge funds were ready for venture capital.

# Chapter 3

# The Seeding Business

The most important cause of growth for the hedge fund industry was the collapse of the internet bubble in 2001 and 2002. Throughout the 1990s hedge funds had continued to grow while remaining largely the preserve of private banks and their clients. Chase's Capital Markets Investment Program (CMIP) program was relatively unusual in putting institutional capital directly into hedge funds. In fact, during the very strong equity markets of the late 1990s leading up to the peak in 2000, we often heard hedge fund managers complain that consistently strong equity market returns were making their hedged, more conservatively run strategies look quite anemic by comparison. The collapse of Long Term Capital Management (LTCM) turned out to be a mere blip along the way, and investors soon concluded that rather than exposing systemic risk it was simply a case of some very smart people with oversized egos. While hedge funds generated acceptable returns, albeit lagging the equity markets through 1999, from 2000 to 2002 they genuinely added value. In the first three years of the new millennium the compounded return on the S&P 500 was −37 percent while hedge funds (as measured by HFR Global Hedge Fund Index [HFRX]) generated a compound return of +30 percent. Hedging was no longer dragging down performance, and most hedge funds clearly fulfilled their promises to protect capital while investors' equity holdings fell sharply.

## How a Venture Capitalist Looks at Hedge Funds

In 2001 I had a series of discussions with John O'Connor around the whole area of hedge funds and institutional interest in them. John was at the time one of the four executive partners within JPMorgan Chase's private equity business. John is a mercurial character; born into a wealthy family, he owned several horses and his free time was dedicated to racing them and hunting. He's highly intelligent and one of the most spontaneously quick-witted people I've ever met. Any meeting with John would invariably include two or three hysterical observations or comments of his that served to lighten the atmosphere and relax the participants. He was unpredictable though, and would literally disappear from contact for days at a time, not responding to e-mails or voicemails. Then he would suddenly respond to an e-mail, arrange a meeting of key participants for the next day, and seemingly swoop down out of the sky with opinions on business strategy for the subject at hand, which he breezily shared with his earthbound colleagues before cutting the meeting short to rush somewhere else.

When I worked for John although I enjoyed his company I appreciated that his interest in my business was only sporadic, and I attributed it to the considerable demands on his time from the mezzanine lending business which he also ran. Then I ran into one of the mezzanine guys who assumed that John spent most of his time with me since they rarely saw him. I never figured out where he was most of the time, and eventually he left after falling out with some of the other partners. I always enjoyed meeting with him though, and while he didn't put much into the execution of our business plan, he was a clearheaded strategic thinker.

John believed that the equity collapse unfolding at the time would lead many institutions to sharply increase their allocations to hedge funds. Many of the best hedge funds already restricted their size and limited the amount of new capital that they would accept. We anticipated an increase in demand for hedge funds that would not be easily accommodated by the industry in its existing state. As we thought through the implications and how we might develop a business around this, we settled on a plan to provide early stage financing, or *seed* capital, to new hedge fund managers. By tapping into JPMorgan's vast network we felt we could identify some of the best new hedge fund managers and provide them with early funding on preferential terms that would give us participation in their businesses.

Investors often like to wait and observe a new manager for several months before committing capital. We calculated that our early investment would allow the manager to develop a track record while he awaited other clients. When the later investors did ultimately commit, the manager's business growth would drive up our investment return through our share in his growing revenues from fees. In addition smaller, newer hedge funds were widely believed to do better than more established funds, which we felt should help our results.

The plan required more detail and crucially depended on our ability to negotiate deals with talented managers, but it was a sound strategy and many others followed in our footsteps in later years. We agreed to move ahead together. Now we needed some capital of our own to get started. "We have $50 million, let's go with that." said John as he breezily left another meeting before its final conclusion. Insightful on strategy, weak on detail. I'd already had an analyst carry out extensive financial modeling to forecast possible returns to the seeding strategy and to measure its sensitivity to the main variables, which were the performance of each hedge fund, their rate of business growth, and the economics of our deal with them. Our base case, or middle of the road assumption, was that a hedge fund would require a $25 million investment from us to get started, would make 8 percent per year, and would gain clients at a rate of approximately $100 million in assets under management (AUM) per year.

After five years the manager would be managing more than $600 million in client assets and our likely return on investment would be about 15 to 16 percent (the 8 percent hedge fund return plus a chunk of the manager's fees from all the other clients). This was an attractive return, and if the manager's business grew faster than we expected, our returns could increase dramatically. But a key component was the initial $25 million to start the fund. We knew from our research that $5 to $10 million wouldn't be enticing enough to attract the quality of traders we were looking for. The price of admission was $25 million, and John had managed to get his partners in the private equity business to ante up enough for only two deals. This was not nearly enough to build a diversified portfolio of hedge funds, for which I estimated we'd need at least $200 million. As I pointed out the inadequacy of the money to John, he told me to visit Andy Craighead who would "sort something out." With that brief instruction the next year of my life was booked.

## From Concept to the Real Deal

Andy Craighead was a JPMorgan lifer, having spent his entire career there, working in the private bank that provided banking and investment services to many of the world's wealthiest people. JPMorgan's Private Bank operated out of a separate building on Park Avenue, and everything about them exuded a culture of old money, excellent taste, and good upbringing. The people were invariably well mannered and attractive, and immediately made you feel at ease. The trading desks at least appeared to be cherry or mahogany, and the conference rooms were often furnished with expensive-looking art or lined with books. Waiters would appear to refill silver pitchers with iced water or bring lunch on fine china. The whole atmosphere was somehow timeless and unhurried, all designed to project safety of capital, combined with exclusive opportunity for their wealthy clients, while quietly extracting healthy fees.

Andy fitted very comfortably into this world. He has the slim build of a cyclist and every comment is both carefully considered and usually insightful. Andy was in the business of developing new investment products for JPMorgan's wealthy clients, and he was going to help us develop our hedge fund seeding concept into something that would attract clients to invest alongside JPMorgan's $50 million. I had no idea how complex and time consuming it would be just to raise the money in order to start investing it. To that point in my career I had only ever managed proprietary capital; the steps required as a fiduciary to develop an investment process and legal structure that would pass through the approval process were as yet unknown to me, although the education I received navigating the project through was invaluable. Suffice it to say Andy was a fantastic partner who combined a quick understanding of our investment idea with sound judgment on how to turn it into an investable product that clients would find attractive. He delved into details that I couldn't have anticipated and although it took many months to complete, the result was a robust investment model with a sound legal structure.

So we set about meeting with potential hedge fund managers. Over the years that we ran this program we considered around 3,500 proposals from managers looking for seed capital. I had two key partners who worked with me on all the deals. Andreas Deutschmann is the strong, silent type. His obsession with detail reflected his German ancestry, and while Andreas is not shy, he uses words sparingly. I came to value his reliability and thoroughness as we waded through dozens of hedge fund presentations every month in our search for the less than 1 percent with whom we would ultimately invest. Miles Doherty was my CFO and looked into all the operational aspects of the managers we considered. Miles loved the opportunity new businesses allow to be involved in multiple tasks, and over time his skills easily expanded from his accounting background to include trading operations, reviewing legal documents, and handling background checks. Eventually we gave up some of the independence afforded us in JPMorgan's entrepreneurial private equity division and moved into the Asset Management division. While this allowed us to operate more efficiently, it made Miles' job less interesting by reassigning parts of it, and he ultimately moved on to another startup.

I'd always ask a new manager what they were looking for in a strategic partner, which is how we thought of ourselves. The answers might include business advice, risk management software, operating infrastructure, but always included money. That is the essence of the seeding relationship. How much AUM will the manager gain through giving up part of his business to JPMorgan? There was the capital we would invest at the outset; the further capital that it was hoped we'd raise for the manager through JPMorgan's extensive client network; and the other money that would presumably follow as investors concluded a JPMorgan seeded manager had presumably received the equivalent of the Good Housekeeping Seal of Approval.

It's all about the money, and AUM growth fuelled by strong returns was the goal. In a typical proposal, we'd offer $25 million of capital in exchange for 25 percent of the business. The business share would come, not through a direct equity stake in the manager's company, but through carving off 25 percent of the fees earned from all the other clients. While some managers balked at relinquishing any equity in their startup, the economics can be very attractive to the manager. If, in exchange for 25 percent of his business, he raises 25 percent more in AUM than he otherwise would, he's broken even. Given how quickly investors can flock to an appealing fund, it's a quite plausible scenario. We preferred taking a percentage of revenues over an equity stake for many reasons.

There were tax considerations (too complicated to go into but this structure was uniformly preferred by our tax experts), means of exit (if you own equity in a small hedge fund manager, your ultimate exit opportunities through a sale are limited), and simplicity (earning a piece of the "top line," before expenses, meant not having to worry about whether the manager's tastes included first class business travel or an office in the GM building in New York). As somebody once said to me, we were doing deals the Hollywood way, where movie profits are shared based on revenues from distribution rather than net profit. My negotiating style is to end with both sides feeling as if they've won something. I want the counterparty to be interested in doing another deal one day, as opposed to squeezing every last concession out of someone. In some cases it might have been possible to extract a higher percentage out of a manager keen to do business with us, but I always felt that if ultimately he was successful, he'd grow resentful about the unfair split and we'd spend a great deal of time in distracting arguments.

There's also the adverse selection problem, a very real issue in the seeding business, in that the most talented managers don't require seed capital at all. They are able to fund a start-up with their own personal assets, or are so well respected in the industry that investors flock to them at the outset while capacity still exists. We were looking for the manager who was just a notch below the true stars, almost but not quite able to start without seed capital. Over the years we frequently debated this "quality discount." How far below the gold standard were we willing to go in order to identify someone we'd like to partner with? Of course there's no easy yardstick for this, but we were keenly aware of the zone in which we were operating.

When we started seeding hedge funds in 2001, there were very few others in that business. However, it's an alluring notion to try and seed the next Louis Bacon or Paul Jones, and it wasn't long before many competitors started appearing. Some were dedicated pools of money like ours, while others were hedge fund investors who could make seed investments opportunistically. Then any big hedge fund had the capability to seed a talented trader deciding to go out on his own. Many did, and, as the availability of capital increased, we found ourselves considering managers that, while good, had a blemish somewhere (such as a prior period of weak performance or perhaps a disinterest in the business elements of running a hedge fund).

## Searching for That Rare Gem

We began looking at managers outside the United States, and at one point even considered opportunities in India and Japan. Recently at a lunch I sat next to a manager of a small hedge fund that was investing in global equities. I was interested in where he was finding the best opportunities. "India" was his confident reply. It turned out he'd never been to India but was finding some compelling opportunities amongst small-cap stocks.

From the safety of a developed western economy like the United States where access to, say, clean running water isn't most people's concern and CNBC brings every financial market to your attention, small-cap Indian stocks can look only slightly more exotic than investing in renewable energy. But it's worth visiting places you're thinking of putting your money before placing any bets. As I found out during meetings with Indian hedge fund managers in Mumbai, hundreds of listed stocks on the two Indian stock exchanges trade by appointment only. They may go for days without a trade. They are in most respects private equity, other than the fact that the securities are registered with the Indian regulator.

As I spent more time researching the Indian market and meeting with many participants the veil began to lift. I had a very revealing conversation with one manager who confided in me how they make money. He and two other managers would agree to buy an obscure and illiquid stock through pre-arranged trades. Ajit buys 500,000 shares of XYZ at 100 Rupees from Bipin and then sells them on to Chandran at 125 Rupees. Chandran then completes the loop by selling the 500,000 shares at 150 Rupees back to Bipin. Shares have changed hands at successively higher prices in sizeable volume, something my friend noted would "attract the New York hedge funds."

Like the Venus Flytrap, a carnivorous flower that digests unwitting insects once trapped by its closing leaves, the New York buyer's arrival at 200 Rupees quickly stops the music and the trap closes; Bipin dumps his stock at double the original price and the locals share their gains.

Whether this story is true or not, its telling illustrates that the world is a diverse place and preventing stock manipulation is not as high a public policy objective in some countries as we might think. I once had a discussion with a member of SEBI, the Securities and Exchange Board of India (equivalent to our SEC). I asked him how many insider trading convictions there were in a year. "Oh none," he confidently assured me. "There is no insider trading in India." Oh right, how silly of me to ask.

The trips I made to Mumbai and New Delhi were memorable. Nobody can be unmoved by the dozens of homeless children that surround you in the airport parking lot following a 2 a.m. arrival, the hundreds of people camped out on roadsides or the exquisite judgment possessed by drivers weaving in and out of traffic with aplomb. The contrasts between rich and poor must be as sharp as anywhere in the world. You walk past people begging for just enough to subsist on and into air conditioned offices to discuss investments. In between meetings and on weekends, learning a little about the history and culture of this old country was an unexpected bonus. The desire to succeed evidenced at every level of society assures that India will transform itself in the decades ahead, although weak infrastructure, bureaucracy, and corruption remain formidable barriers and compare unfavorably with China. But I liked the Indian people I met, and I wouldn't bet against them.

Although we met many interesting and talented managers in India, we didn't invest. It's one thing to seed a manager a few blocks away on Park Avenue where you can walk over and discuss exactly how he's lost 10 percent of your investment. Long distance investing requires greater certainty, and for a seed deal with a small manager we were naturally cautious. It is to the eternal credit of my former partners and investment committee colleagues that we maintained our investment criteria at a consistent standard throughout. As a result, we ran out of compelling places to invest our capital, and by 2006 we told our clients we wouldn't be deploying their remaining capital and would be returning what we had. By the time the credit crisis of 2007 and 2008 rolled around we had limited exposure—not because we had foreseen the crash, but because we had the discipline to stay true to our investment objectives. Napoleon famously wanted generals that were lucky. We didn't claim to be smart enough to see what was coming, but maybe we were lucky and that can work just as well as being smart.

Our typical revenue share was structured as a *Preferred Return*. This meant that we only shared in the fees as long as the hedge fund was profitable, and served to satisfy tax considerations raised by our ever-present tax advisors. In fact, it's amazing how much taxes and minimizing them can figure in the seeding business. One consequence was that we had to remain passive investors, which is to say that we couldn't provide any services to our seeded hedge funds. Some people were surprised as they learned how our strategic partnership simply boiled down to the provision of seed capital, because venture capital investors routinely sit on the boards of the companies they finance and provide wide-ranging support as they nurture their startup. However, in our case the passive nature sat very well; the best hedge fund managers understand that they are running an investment portfolio as well as running a business. Both have to be done well for the enterprise to be successful. Ultimately we were going to make our best returns investing with managers who could master both skills, which is how things turned out. A hedge fund manager who was disinterested or unskilled in the business side might think a strategic partner was the solution, but he was really better suited to simply work at a larger hedge fund as an employee. Evidence of poor business planning was usually a sufficient reason for us to reject an opportunity.

Another feature important to most managers was the stability of the capital we invested. They'd want to know that we wouldn't run at the first disappointing month, that we were really committed to the long-term success of the business. These were fair issues, since the manager was often taking significant personal financial risk not only through leaving a well-paid job, but also in spending money on salaries, rent, legal fees, computers, and many other items. Start-up expenses of $1 to $2 million is not uncommon for even a modestly sized hedge fund, before fees from clients can get the business to break even. The stability of the seed capital was therefore a key consideration. Mindful of this, we had asked our investors to make long-term commitments of the capital they entrusted to us, so that we could make similar commitments to our managers.

Our early deals involved a fairly standard two-year lockup on our investment. However, new funds can be risky and we weren't willing to agree to have our money tied up for two years under any circumstances. We might see a manager lose 25 percent after a year, conclude investing in him was an error, and be unable to leave while he continued to lose our money. The obvious solution was to agree on contingencies under which our capital could be released from its lockup. This was usually fairly easy.

Most managers, when you ask them how much we should be willing to lose before deciding that our choice of manager was wrong would respond with a figure between 5 and 15 percent. Few would suggest that we could possibly lose more than 15 percent, though sometimes a statistically minded individual might note that larger losses were possible with decreasing probability. But in most cases, if a manager said down 10 percent was the worst we should expect, it wasn't hard to suggest a release on the capital lockup if this was breached. It's wholly reasonable to let your client out if you've done worse than you ever thought possible, though in 2008 many managers saw fit to impede clients' withdrawals from their funds, often to pre- serve their own businesses. We soon refined 10 percent to be tighter at the outset of the two-year lockup (i.e., if you lose 5 percent in the first month we'd be very disappointed) and toward the end (i.e., if you're not at least profitable after 18 months, the long-term prospects won't be that good). We felt that this set of protections would allow us to agree to lock up our capital under most circumstances, and if an early exit was triggered, then the hedge fund was probably doomed in any case.

But then we learned a little more about human nature. Place your- self for a moment in the seat of a new hedge fund manager. Your seed capital is secure, you've hired a couple of people, rented office space, bought computers and spent anywhere from $50,000 to $250,000 on legal documents for your hedge fund. The first couple of months were bright—your prime broker arranged a number of meetings, there are many potential investors watching your performance from a distance, and you've had two modestly positive months. Incidentally, the advice prime brokers often give new hedge fund managers is to follow two rules: 1, don't lose money in the first few months, and 2, don't forget rule 1. Then markets turn, investing becomes more difficult, and three months later, performance is negative. You're down 6 percent, and suddenly the seed provider's early exit trigger is only 4 percent away. It's at this point that the interests of the hedge fund manager and the seed provider start to diverge. The hedge fund manager can adopt one of two strategies to try and save his vulnerable business. He can decide that losing his seed capital is tantamount to losing his business, along with everything he's invested in it. Accordingly, he dials down risk and becomes ultra-cautious, since his primary objective is to not lose an additional 4 percent that may result in closure.

The subsequent returns are unlikely to be that exciting, and the seed provider may find that they have capital that's locked up and earning a very low return, an expensive Treasury bill, while the manager tries to nurse his performance carefully away from the precipice. The manager's second strategy is to conclude that he'll avoid a slow death and will instead dial risk up, reasoning that he needs high returns to create a sufficiently large performance cushion. This is also not a great outcome for the seed investor, since ideally the level of risk the manager is taking should be determined by his investment research and the quality of the opportunities he's identified rather than a Las Vegas style assessment of likely payoff. At its worst this is known as the *airport trade*. You buy an enormous amount of something that you think will go up in price (Apple stock, currency futures, call options on crude oil). You use an imprudent amount of leverage. In short, you risk everything. You also buy a one-way plane ticket to Rio de Janeiro. At the airport before boarding you call to check on how the trade has worked out. If it's a winner you take a cab back home. If it's a loser you get on that plane. This was not a scenario we wanted to encourage.

The seed investor could impose risk limits that would prevent the latter course by the manager, but in practice these can be extremely complex to negotiate and traders can always lose more money than even a robust set of risk limits would permit. Fortunately, we had a manager who chose the low-risk option of the two described above, and as our investment began looking like a bank CD minus 2 and 20, we negotiated an amicable parting of the ways.

## Everybody Has a Story

After this we never locked up our capital, and, when explained this way, most managers understood the potential for a divergence of interests. Instead, recognizing that the secure fees associated with locked-up capital were almost as important as the capital itself, we separated the two. While we retained the right to withdraw our capital on the same terms as any other investor in the hedge fund, we committed to pay management fees for at least two years under any circumstances. Indeed, in some cases we varied from the common 1 to 2 percent management fee and 20 percent performance fee with a higher management fee (3 percent or even 4 percent) and a commensurately lower incentive fee (10 percent or maybe as little as 5 percent of profits). Guaranteed fee revenue has high value to most new businesses, and the lower incentive share meant that the manager only needed to achieve an average return for our overall fees to be lower.

Investors assume business risk whenever they invest in a hedge fund. In a very real sense they need the hedge fund manager to run a successful business in order for their investment in him to be worthwhile. This is not the same as fraud risk, it's a recognition that if the manager doesn't generate adequate compensation to make the business successful, he will eventually close up shop. Many investors focus their operational due diligence on ensuring that valuations are accurate, that trade settlement is secure, that multiple signatures are required to move funds, and so on. In doing so they are concerned that the day-to-day operations of the fund are robust enough to minimize errors or catch dishonest behavior. This is operational risk. Business risk is the possibility that the manager's enterprise may fail—and it doesn't require significant investment losses for that to happen.

Even mediocre returns can cause the investor base to shrink and threaten the viability of the manager's firm. In the case of established hedge funds, many investors no doubt conclude that reaching a certain threshold of, say, $1 billion in AUM is sufficient proof of the manager's business acumen. But, in the case of new and emerging hedge fund managers, evaluating business risk is an important element of the investor's overall due diligence. Some of the strongest proposals we evaluated included a written business plan describing the investment strategy, the potential market, key service providers, sources and uses of working capital, and a timeline for growth. Inevitably the projections were overly optimistic, but at least the existence of a business plan showed that the manager recognized the twin objectives of running a portfolio and running an asset-management business successfully.

On one occasion we met with a young guy in his late 20s who was running a very small long/short equity hedge fund of around $5 million. He had a Harvard MBA, and had come to us looking for seed capital to boost his AUM to a level at which institutional investors might start to follow his track record. As he began his presentation he moved easily into his well-worn dissertation about screening hundreds of stocks based on his specific criteria. He further explained that he'd researched a select few more deeply, evaluating their business models, how they were implementing their business plans, and their overall growth prospects. It was the same, generic description we'd heard hundreds of times, and as I listened to him, I wondered how much thought he'd given to his own business.

So I asked him what his plan was to grow his firm. And this freshly minted Harvard MBA was momentarily confused—this wasn't a typical question. He was used to describing individual stocks he'd researched and explaining how some insight of his had uncovered something that the markets had missed, something of previously unrecognized value. Quickly regaining his composure but clearly without having considered the question before, he responded simply that he planned to generate good returns upon which he expected investors would start to show up. This is called the *Field of Dreams* strategy, after the 1989 Kevin Costner movie in which an Iowa farmer builds a baseball diamond in his cornfield because he heard voices whispering, "If you build it, they will come." And, being Hollywood, a baseball team did duly arrive. But our erstwhile hedge fund manager was a gangly and somewhat nervous young man who didn't look much like Kevin Costner. So I couldn't resist the opening, and I pointed out that while he was busy evaluating other companies' business plans and their execution ability, he had failed to develop one for his own business. Unable to pass up such an easy target, I paused before adding, "And on top of that, you're a Harvard MBA." It was entertaining, but obviously not a profitable way to spend our time. We quickly wound up the discussion and wished him well.

A surprising number of proposals came to us consisting of two people operating as co-portfolio managers (PMs). No doubt there is welcome security in starting a new business venture with a trusted friend. There's certainly nothing wrong with having business partners and any successful hedge fund starts life with a number of key people already identified to oversee portfolio management, research, trading, business development, and infrastructure. But whenever we saw two people who planned to share responsibility for the portfolio, a red flag went up, particularly if they'd never worked together before. While successful investing almost always involves multiple people with complementary skills, hedge funds employ leverage and they require crisp decision making that does not lend itself well to the natural give and take of a discussion with a partner. Very few successful hedge funds have co-PMs at the top. Joint decision making by its very nature requires discussion and compromise.

Often investing and trading require doing things that are against the prevailing consensus in the market place. Groups and investment committees can be extremely good at making strategic decisions: deciding on issues that are important but don't require an immediate decision; how much capital to allocate to equities over the next five years; whether to invest in merger arbitrage; long-term return assumptions on a set of asset classes for a pension fund. These are examples of issues about which a group of informed investment professionals with diverse experiences can make decisions that are better than what an individual may conclude. They are important, but not urgent, and can be discussed over multiple meetings, if necessary, to flesh out all the considerations.

On the other hand, if two people have to agree on whether to buy a stock now or tomorrow or next week, the result can be a time-consuming and unsatisfactory compromise that ultimately doesn't reflect the preference of either individual. At times I've managed traders who might have opposite positions in the same security. While the risks would cancel out across the trading division as a whole, each trader would have a different reason for holding that position and often they'd both make money through buying and selling at different times from one another. Similarly, there can be many good ways to enter and exit a position, and I'm always skeptical that co-PMs are going to do a better job than either one of them. In fact, for the seed investor, evaluating co-PMs who have not managed a portfolio together can be virtually impossible.

We met one pair who both had quite respectable but independent track records from their prior jobs. They were proposing to combine their investment skill with a $2 + 2 = 5$ type of outcome. But the problem for us was that we didn't know if $2 + 2$ would even equal 4. It might even be negative, because they'd never worked together. When we asked them why they were planning to share responsibility for running the portfolio, they responded that they'd been friends for years, discussed markets together on a regular basis, and felt that their common philosophy made them a perfect match. Maybe it did—the problem was that when you combine two investment processes and include the need for joint decision making, nobody really knows what the ultimate outcome will look like.

In practice it will be a third, new investment process, an outcome of the first two but not simply the sum of the best features and an elimination of the worst. In fact, from an investor's standpoint, judging just the track record without considering the other features of the new hedge fund, it was a much simpler decision to allocate $10 million to each of them individually, based on their individual past performance, than to invest in their new and unproven investment model. But they were both leaving much larger firms and preferred the security of pooling their resources in order to work together.

So the obvious question was, "I understand why it's good for you both to be co-PMs and work together in this new business, but why is it better for the investor that you do it this way? Why aren't we better off giving you each half of the money?" And there's really no good answer to this question, because there's no past performance that's relevant and can be used to try and evaluate the future. This particular meeting ended poorly when one of the two would-be co-PMs huffed that many investors had asked them to set it up just this way, and therefore it ought to be good enough for JPMorgan. The fact that they were meeting with us to raise seed capital for their not-yet-launched fund cast some doubt on the strength of investor support for this statement, as I pointed out.

However, sometimes we passed up opportunities that turned out to be good, and in this instance it should be noted that the co-PMs did indeed launch successfully. When I looked at their returns and AUM growth some years later, they had evidently been nicely profitable, and no doubt they looked back with satisfaction at our misplaced skepticism at the time. Nonetheless, they were the exception, and it's certainly true today that co-PMs are a rare breed amongst successful hedge funds.

## Some Things Shouldn't Be Hedged

Master Limited Partnerships (MLPs) are investments in energy infrastructure businesses, such as pipelines, storage facilities, and refining plants. Because they're not organized as corporations, they don't pay corporate income tax which means their owners avoid the double taxation common with most equity investments (i.e., dividends on a stock are paid out of a company's after tax profits, and the investor is then himself subject to paying tax on the dividend received). MLPs pay dividends (they're called distributions) without deducting corporate income tax, which makes them attractive investments. Their unique tax structure limits them to wealthy investors willing to deal with some complicated tax reporting but many high-net-worth investors have found them attractive and interest continues to grow.

MLPs are good investments that belong in most portfolios above a certain size. Over time they generate reliable returns. They don't need hedging, or leverage, or the use of options or any complicated strategies placed on top of them. They're solid long-term investments and there's not much gain in adding complexity. Sometimes simple is better.

However, in 2004 when we were looking for new strategies we started considering MLPs as a potential area if we could find the right manager. After a couple of false starts we did come across a young man called Gabriel Hammond with his new hedge fund Alerian. All the managers we seriously considered were at least in their late 30s and had 15 years or more trading experience. When we first met Gabe we sat across a table from this 20-something analyst recently of Goldman Sachs who looked even younger than his years and appeared slightly ill at ease. I didn't think it likely we'd invest with someone so young, and quickly inflicted my mediocre humor on him by asking what he'd learned trading through the (still recent) dot-com collapse. "Oh, but of course, you were still in school," I cut him off before letting him reply. Finally I did let Gabe tell his story and out poured a highly articulate dissertation of MLPs supported with numerous facts and figures all provided without any reference to notes. I was impressed. You learn a lot more by listening than talking.

We went through our exhaustive due diligence process over the next few months and Alerian's long/short fund became one of our seed investments. The strategy was fairly straightforward—go long MLPs that appeared undervalued and hedge the risk by shorting MLPs that were overvalued. Although hedge funds hadn't been active MLP investors in the past, the growth in the industry led to many unexplored sectors receiving scrutiny and as a result several other MLP hedge funds began to appear at the same time.

Sharing in the fees that Alerian generated from other clients as their business grew turned out to be the best part of the deal for us, because by 2007/8 markets turned and MLP hedge funds managed to lose more than MLPs themselves. That's right, in many cases their results were worse than if an investor had simply owned MLPs and not bothered to hedge them at all. In a classic crowded trade, the undervalued MLPs were the small, riskier ones and the overvalued MLPs were the big, reliable cash-flow generators. Most hedge funds had similar positions (there weren't that many different MLPs available to trade) and the cheap ones become far cheaper while the expensive ones remained expensive. Leverage performed its magic on this sorry brew and there aren't many MLP hedge funds left.

One MLP fund I was following managed to lose an eye-popping 80 percent in 2008, through increasing their bad bets directly following the collapse of Lehman. Their salesman even had the chutzpah to call asking if we'd consider an investment. MLPs were cheap, but someone who'd lost four fifths of their clients' money couldn't be relied upon to save the last fifth.

Alerian struggled with the rest of them and reoriented their business to focus on long only investing, (KISS—keep it simple, stupid!) and their eponymous index business. MLPs remain attractive investments— they just shouldn't be hedged. Sharing in Alerian's fees certainly made our own results more acceptable than they would have been as a regular investor. Once again, we'd learned that the returns from a hedge fund manager's business are better than from a hedge fund.

## The Hedge Fund as a Business

We built a financial model to illustrate what types of returns we could generate by seeding hedge funds. In a sense we were venture capital (VC) investors, providing the first financing for a new business. VC investing usually results in a large number of losses with just a handful of successful investments generating a profit. Often just one or two wildly successful investments in startups such as Google or Facebook will more than offset 30 or more failures. Failures in VC investing usually result in a complete loss of capital, while successes can generate returns of 100 times the original amount invested. Although we understood the analogy between providing seed to hedge funds with venture capital investing, we believed the range of outcomes would be far narrower.

We hardly expected to make even 10 times our investment with any hedge fund, and while we obviously expected losses, we thought it unlikely we'd suffer a complete loss. Indeed, to lose all your money in a hedge fund requires fraud—or such utter incompetence that it would be gross negligence. We always negotiated direct and independent access to all the positions a hedge fund held, so that we could verify everything without the intervention of the hedge fund manager. Because fraud is so catastrophic we were obsessive about protecting ourselves. As I recount in Chapter 8, almost anybody can surprise you and we took nothing for granted. Fortunately, we did not invest in a fraud although we weren't always happy with some of the decisions managers made.

In our financial model we recognized that we'd invest in some clunkers, and we assumed they would lose 20 percent of our capital on average before we could withdraw our investment. As it turned out, failures were much less expensive. The funds that ultimately failed lost in aggregate less than 5 percent of our capital. In fact, most hedge funds that close are business failures rather than investment failures. Although the spectacular losses are the ones that grab the headlines, in our experience far more hedge funds just withered and died because their returns were boring so they couldn't attract any investors. We struggled much more with managers who were overly cautious in their early trading.

The large Wall Street investment banks provide prime brokerage services to hedge funds, which offer financing of positions, borrowed stock for shorts, trade execution and settlement, and capital introduction services. "Cap intro" involves the bank introducing potential clients to the new hedge fund. Since bigger hedge funds are more profitable clients for the bank's prime broker division, there is plenty of motivation for the banks to guide investors to their hedge fund clients. However, the regulations around hedge fund marketing and the legal liability for the banks are both so onerous that everybody involved signs forms agreeing that no actual marketing is going on, that nobody's recommending anything, and that hedge funds are very risky.

Because no fees are charged directly for prime broking services, it's always hard to figure out how effective it is. An investor might meet a hedge fund at several such events before investing, so it's rarely easy to attribute new capital to a particular meeting. One thing prime brokers do impress upon their new hedge fund clients is that early performance is critical and sharp losses potentially fatal. It's not unreasonable advice, and many entrepreneurs no doubt instinctively feel that way anyway. But it does mean that a new manager can die slowly, a death caused by many unspectacular months of performance, while he assiduously avoids taking the kinds of risks that can generate eye-catching gains if they pay off.

I had an interesting discussion with one new hedge fund manager that illustrates the quandary. The fund had been trading for a year, and were still managing just our seed capital and their own. Returns had been lackluster but by no means poor, and many potential investors were on their mailing list (meaning they were theoretically receiving monthly performance updates if they opened the relevant e-mails). As a business, running a hedge fund provides tremendous optionality. The business downside can be controlled, since the start-up costs need not be that high. It's not necessary to build a fabrication plant to manufacture a new widget, or invest millions in researching a new drug.

The investment required is largely working capital to operate the business at a loss, for however long it takes to attract enough clients or to conclude it's not going to be a success. And, as is well known, financial success can be enormous, since hedge fund managers possess very high operating leverage. They have scalable business models, in that clients can be added without necessarily increasing overhead. At the same time, the investment results, which are the product, need to be sufficiently high to attract attention and ultimately money.

The business value of a hedge fund's management company looks very like a call option; it has a cost limited to the cumulative operating

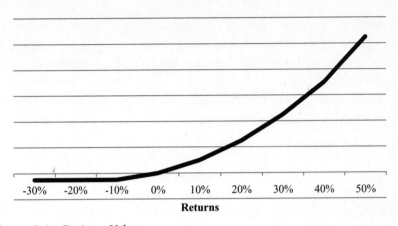

**Figure 3.1**   Business Value

expenses of the firm, and a potential value that can appear virtually limitless if the investment results are high enough. The chart in Figure 3.1 illustrates the point. The hedge fund manager's business has virtually no value if average returns don't reach an acceptable level, such as 10 percent. Generating 6 percent, 3 percent, 0 percent, or losing money all result in a business venture with the same negative value (equal to the cumulative operating costs). A 6 percent return if achieved with very little risk may appear to be a great start. We often met with managers who would describe such returns as "high quality" in that they'd been achieved with great consistency. Their volatility was low, or they had a high Sharpe Ratio. This is of little use. A strategy with a high Sharpe Ratio can presumably have leverage added to it in order to increase the returns.

The manager marketing his 6 percent return as high quality is in effect suggesting that the investor should regard a potential investment as less risky than another hedge fund, or perhaps even leverage it himself. But, of course, if the manager's risk is really that low, he's the one who should increase it, presumably generating the higher returns of which his strategy is capable. But another reason is that 6 percent in many years just won't stand out. It's not eye catching and it's unlikely to attract many investors. So in practice, any return less than 10 percent will result in the same value of the manager's new business. It will be worth zero, minus the costs already incurred. Either +6 percent or −6 percent returns will ultimately lead to closure of the business (although obviously to the provider of the initial capital in the fund, which might very well be only the manager himself, making versus losing 6 percent will matter).

# Summary

What we and others who followed us had done was to begin the transformation of hedge funds from a cottage industry servicing wealthy individuals and a handful of sophisticated institutions to a fairly conventional add-on to traditional portfolio management. The strong returns of the 1990s during a bull market followed by the bear market of 2000 to 2002 (when hedge funds demonstrated their hedging ability to great effect) eventually brought them to the attention of virtually every institutional investor in the world. Venture capital investors try to anticipate game-changing products or services that alter the landscape forever by fulfilling a need that didn't previously exist. Most investors didn't know they needed hedge funds until the tech bubble collapsed. During subsequent years many looked at the industry's returns and decided that their portfolios would be incomplete without hedge funds.

How hedge funds made money for clients remained opaque though. In fact, one of the most reliable comments in any meeting with a manager is that they don't easily fit in one category or another and that their returns and risk just don't look quite like anything else. Something that makes money most of the time and doesn't lose money when your other investments are going down is highly valuable. Like a car that never needs refueling, or a light bulb that never burns out, it's easy for the buyer to think that they almost can't overpay for such a rare creation. "Absolute, uncorrelated returns" are virtually the holy grail for investors. The word "absolute" means they're not negative, and "uncorrelated" means they'll zig when other assets zag. Combining different assets in such a way as to achieve this happy result is the goal of every long-term investor.

We knew people would pay a great deal of money for this—on a relatively small scale they already were. Everybody understood that running a successful hedge fund was a path to the very highest reaches of wealth, so it was already obvious that the business of hedge funds could be very, very good. But even we didn't foresee just how effectively the concept of absolute, uncorrelated returns in the hands of smart, highly commercial people could lead to such a transfer of wealth to the hedge fund industry from its clients.

# Chapter 4

# Where Are the Customers' Yachts?

A nalyzing hedge fund industry performance isn't as simple as it should be. For a start, there are several indices whose results can vary quite widely from month to month and their construction isn't uniform either. For the analysis in Chapter 1, I used the HFR Global Hedge Fund Index (HFRX), which is an asset-weighted index, meaning that the return of each hedge fund is weighted by the size of that hedge fund in calculating the result. It makes sense to use such an index when assessing how investors as a whole have done, but each choice has shortcomings. Hedge funds report their results voluntarily and not all choose to disclose their size, which means only those managers willing to provide both figures can be included in HFRX.

All indices suffer from voluntary reporting, and survivor bias is a well-known problem with reported returns. Since only successful funds are going to report, a fund can easily choose to stop reporting during a string of bad results. In addition, some indices incur *backfill bias*; when adding a new fund to a benchmark, some index providers will "fill in" prior months' results with the (presumably positive) results of the fund. There is plenty of academic research which seeks to estimate how much the widely used indices are distorted by this effect. Generally, estimates are in the 3 to 5 percent range (Dichev, 2009), meaning that actual results experienced by investors are probably lower than the reported indices by this amount. None of the indices referred to in this book have been modified to reflect survivor bias or backfill bias, so any overstatement of returns in those indices remains. This means that the results could be even worse for investors, but the discrepancy between what the industry has paid itself compared to what its clients have earned is already so vast that it hardly alters the overall story.

## How Much Profit Is There Really?

Everybody knows the top hedge fund managers earn vast sums of money. One can debate whether the most successful managers, athletes, or actresses deserve what they get paid, but the marketplace rewards exceptional talent and always will. Frankly, after hearing John Paulson describe his enormously successful investments against sub-prime mortgages it's hard not to admire the fresh perspective he brought and his unshakeable conviction as he bet heavily against almost the entire market. The *Financial Times* reported that since setting up his fund in 1994 John Paulson has made investors $32.2 billion (Mackintosh, 2010), making him the second most profitable hedge fund for clients in history, behind only George Soros at $35 billion (although his sharp reversal in fortunes in 2011 knocked him down the list). Paulson has been handsomely rewarded. The *Financial Times* article in 2010 was based on an unconventional view of hedge funds, highlighted by research carried out by Rick Sopher, chairman of LCH Investments. Rick has calculated how much profit the best hedge funds have made for their clients, the point being that a few dozen have produced most of the investors' returns. The trick is, of course, identifying which ones to invest in before they produce that happy result.

While the fees earned by the top managers are presumably accept-able to their clients, the hedge fund industry in aggregate has pulled off a quite remarkable split of the profits—even more so considering how little investors as a whole have made. It's not that hard to estimate hedge fund industry fees. Given annual assets under management (AUM) data from BarclayHedge and annual returns from whichever index provider one prefers, the standard "2 & 20" (2 percent management fee and 20 percent incentive fee) can be applied, to come up with some reasonable estimates. Not all managers charge a 2 percent management fee—many smaller funds charge 1 percent, and some larger funds charge more. The 20 percent incentive fee is reasonably standard although a profit split of up to 50 percent has been known.

However, estimating fees on the industry as if it's one enormous hedge fund does include one simplification, in that it excludes any netting of positive with negative results. To use a simple example, if an investor's portfolio included two hedge funds whose results cancelled out (one manager was +10 percent while the other was −10 percent) the investor's total return would be 0 percent and for our purposes here we'll assume that no incentive fee was paid on the 0 percent return. However, in reality the profitable manager would still charge an incen-tive fee. It's not possible with the available data to break down the returns to that level of detail, so the fee estimates derived are under-stated, in that it's assumed incentive fees are charged only on the indus-try's aggregate profits, whereas in fact all the profitable managers would have charged incentive fees with no offset from the losing managers. The true picture is worse than the one in Table 4.1, which is already bad enough. The data goes back to 1998, simply because that's when the BarclayHedge series begins. Given how the industry has grown since then though, the overall result wouldn't be very different if earlier data was included.

In assessing how much investors have paid for their hedge fund love affair, there are a couple of ways to look at it. One is to express the fees paid as a percentage of overall assets, which allows easy com-parison with mutual funds. The other is to look at what share of the overall profits are being returned to investors, versus those retained by the industry. In this case, excess profits over Treasury bills is the relevant measure of profits, since in years when the industry has failed to do

**Table 4.1**  Hedge Fund Returns Using HFRX

| Year | Average AUM* (BNs) | HFRX | Real Investor Profits (BNs) | Estimated Total Fees (BNs)** | Fees as Percentage of AUM | Total Profits | Industry Share of Total Profits |
|------|------|------|------|------|------|------|------|
| 1998 | $ 131 | 13% | $ 10 | $ 7 | 5% | $ 17 | 40% |
| 1999 | $ 166 | 27% | $ 36 | $ 14 | 9% | $ 51 | 28% |
| 2000 | $ 213 | 14% | $ 17 | $ 12 | 6% | $ 29 | 41% |
| 2001 | $ 279 | 9% | $ 13 | $ 12 | 4% | $ 25 | 47% |
| 2002 | $ 414 | 5% | $ 12 | $ 13 | 3% | $ 26 | 51% |
| 2003 | $ 666 | 13% | $ 82 | $ 36 | 5% | $118 | 30% |
| 2004 | $1,027 | 3% | $ 14 | $ 27 | 3% | $ 42 | 66% |
| 2005 | $1,295 | 3% | -$ 6 | $ 35 | 3% | $ 29 | 119% |
| 2006 | $1,537 | 9% | $ 67 | $ 66 | 4% | $133 | 50% |
| 2007 | $1,925 | 4% | -$ 11 | $ 59 | 3% | $ 48 | 122% |
| 2008 | $1,797 | -23% | -$448 | $ 36 | 2% | -$412 | NM |
| 2009 | $1,506 | 13% | $200 | $ 30 | 2% | $230 | 13% |
| 2010 | $1,624 | 5% | $ 83 | $ 32 | 2% | $115 | 28% |
| Total | | | $ 70 | $379 | | $449 | 84% |

*SOURCE: BarclayHedge
**Assumes 2 & 20 with no incentive fees after 2008 since so many funds were below their high water marks.

better than the risk-free rate it can hardly claim to have generated any profits. Earning 5 percent when Treasury bills are 2 percent is a 3 percent excess return or profit to the investor, although incentive fees are normally charged on the total return. So the definition of Real Investor Profits used here is the return on hedge funds minus the return that could have been earned by investing in Treasury bills. Table 4.1 shows the results.

As a percentage of AUM, hedge fund fees have actually come down since the late 1990s. The 27 percent return in 1999 when the industry bounced back from the Russian default and collapse of Long Term Capital Management was very strong by any measure, and the normal 20 percent incentive fee led to managers keeping almost 9 percent of AUM. And in fact, the $36 billion of Real Investor Profits earned by investors in 1999 stood as their best-ever result for three years, even while the industry's AUM more than doubled. During the 2000 to 2002 equity bear market, hedge funds really did add value as they preserved capital and this performance led to strong institutional inflows.

But the Industry Share of Total Profits has been growing steadily. To get Total Profits I've added fees back to Real Investor Profits, since the investors' returns have already had fees deducted. Total Profits is how much is made before the managers' fees are deducted. So in 1998 for example, Total Profits were $17BN ($10BN Real Investor Profits + $7BN in Fees) and so the Industry Share of Total Profits was $7BN divided by $17BN, or 40 percent.

The numbers speak for themselves. Since 1998 hedge fund managers have kept 84 percent of the profits, leaving 16 percent for the investors.

## Investors Jump In

By 2003 rebounding markets, combined with a 50 percent increase in AUM, led to the industry's best-ever Real Investor Profits—an estimated $82 billion after fees. Management and incentive fees garnered $36 billion, almost three times the prior year and 30 percent of Total Profits. This also represented the high point for investors, in that profits in subsequent years never reached $82 billion again until 2009, when the industry made back less than half of its losses from the catastrophic prior year. In six years out of 13, the industry's earnings from fees have eclipsed or been roughly equal to the returns of its clients. In three years (2005, 2007, and 2008) it generated billions in fees while its clients lost money. Overall since 1998 fees have totaled $379 billion, compared with Real Investor Profits of $70 billion.

Fees as a percentage of Total Profits is probably the fairest way to assess the split between the industry and its clients. Over the long run, investors in hedge funds are interested in what they've earned in excess of the risk-free alternative and how much they've paid in fees to achieve that. These investment returns are also better if uncorrelated with returns from traditional assets of course, although 2008 established quite clearly that at times of extreme crisis almost all risky strategies suffer together. The net result is that the hedge fund industry has kept more

**Table 4.2**  Hedge Fund Returns Using HFRX Adjusted for Survivor and Backfill Bias

| Year | Average AUM* (BNs) | HFRX −3 Percent (survivor bias) | Real Investor Profits (BNs) | Estimated Total Fees (BNs)** | Fees as Percentage of AUM | Total Profits | Industry Share of Total Profits |
|------|------|------|------|------|------|------|------|
| 1998 | $   131 | 10% | $   6 | $   6 | 4% | $  12 | 48% |
| 1999 | $   166 | 24% | $  31 | $  13 | 8% | $  44 | 30% |
| 2000 | $   213 | 11% | $  11 | $  10 | 5% | $  21 | 48% |
| 2001 | $   279 | 6% | $   5 | $  10 | 3% | $  14 | 66% |
| 2002 | $   414 | 2% | $   0 | $  10 | 2% | $  10 | 100% |
| 2003 | $   666 | 10% | $  62 | $  31 | 5% | $  93 | 33% |
| 2004 | $1,027 | 0% | −$  17 | $  21 | 2% | $   4 | 534% |
| 2005 | $1,295 | 0% | −$  44 | $  26 | 2% | −$  19 | NM |
| 2006 | $1,537 | 6% | $  20 | $  55 | 4% | $  75 | 73% |
| 2007 | $1,925 | 1% | −$  68 | $  44 | 2% | −$  24 | NM |
| 2008 | $1,797 | 0% | −$502 | $  36 | 2% | −$466 | NM |
| 2009 | $1,506 | 10% | $154 | $  30 | 2% | $184 | 16% |
| 2010 | $1,624 | 2% | $  34 | $  32 | 2% | $  66 | 49% |
| **Total** | | | **−$308** | **$324** | | **$  16** | **NM** |

*SOURCE: BarclayHedge
**Assumes no incentive fees, as many funds were still below their high water marks following 2008.

than four-fifths of what they've made in the form of fees, leaving the investors far behind.

As lopsided as this sounds, it's really even worse. The analysis above in Table 4.1 uses HFRX returns without any adjustment for survivor bias or backfill bias, which you'll recall can cause hedge fund returns to be overstated by 3 to 5 percent. If we reduce the annual HFRX returns by 3 percent, the fees drop to $324 billion, but the Real Investor Profits earned fall to *negative $308 billion,* as shown in Table 4.2.

No doubt the thousand-year flood that was 2008 is skewing the result, but even if the industry had been flat that year, Total Profits over this time period would have been $194 billion compared with $324 billion in fees. If the 3 percent adjustment for survivor bias used in Table 4.2 is a true reflection of what's happened, it means that hedge fund managers have kept all the money that's been made, and the investors have in aggregate received nothing. Remember this is simply the total; there are plenty of satisfied hedge fund clients, but the math suggests there must be many more who are unhappy or should be. And Total Profits here is calculated as the excess return over Treasury bills. Whether the HFRX return series is used, or the one adjusted for survivor bias, it's clear that hedge fund managers have been making more from their clients' money than their clients have.

Then there's netting. We're treating the entire industry like one giant hedge fund which charges a 20 percent incentive fee when returns are positive. However hedge funds that lose money don't pay investors (i.e., there's no negative incentive fee) and of course investors are charged incentive fees even when their overall portfolio loses. John Paulson alone was estimated by *Alpha Magazine* to have earned $3.7 billion in 2008 (largely incentive fees but this includes the profits on his own capital). But to keep it simple, and conservative, the calculations above assume that there were no incentive fees charged across the entire industry in 2008 because performance was negative, or during 2009 and 2010 because so many funds were below their high water marks. There's no reasonable way to estimate the effect of this without having the returns of all the individual managers, but not adjusting for this presents the industry in a more favorable light.

## Fees on Top of More Fees

And there's even more. The hedge fund of funds industry takes its cut too, and that's not included yet. All the data above is based on AUM of hedge funds, but around a third of hedge fund investors make their allocations through funds of hedge funds (FOFs). In this way investors outsource the work to firms that are better equipped to handle it. Large FOFs can employ 100 people or more, covering everything from manager research and due diligence, risk management to operations, accounting, and client service. Hedge fund investing is a labor-intensive business. For investors with less than, say, $250 million to invest, it's not worth the expense to develop their own investment staff, so they often farm it out. FOFs charge less than hedge funds, although of course their fees are on top of those charged by the hedge funds themselves. A 1 percent management fee with a 5 to 10 percent incentive fee (sometimes calculated on returns over a given benchmark) is not uncommon. For simplicity's sake, let's assume that FOFs simply charge a 1 percent management fee on the AUM they're managing, with no incentive fee.

For many years the FOF industry's growth tracked that of the hedge fund industry itself, as institutional investors outsourced their allocation decisions. However, one glaring weakness of the FOF model was revealed in 2008, in that just as hedge funds can experience sudden client redemption requests, so can FOFs. As a result, many large hedge funds prefer "direct" investors, since they know they're dealing with the decision maker, rather than third parties such as FOFs, who may themselves experience redemptions that they have to meet. In addition, institutional investors often graduate from the FOF model to establish their own investment teams, thus retaining expertise in-house and reducing the fees they're paying on their capital. Table 4.3 shows that FOFs have earned $61BN on top of what hedge fund managers have received.

**Table 4.3**   Fees Charged by Funds of Hedge Funds

| Year | Average HF AUM* (BNs) | Average FOF AUM (BNs) | FOF Industry as Percent of Total Industry | Estimated FOF Fees (BNs)** |
|------|----------------------|----------------------|------------------------------------------|---------------------------|
| 1998 | $  131 | $   60 | 46% | $  1 |
| 1999 | $  166 | $   74 | 45% | $  1 |
| 2000 | $  213 | $   96 | 45% | $  1 |
| 2001 | $  279 | $  132 | 47% | $  1 |
| 2002 | $  414 | $  179 | 43% | $  2 |
| 2003 | $  666 | $  281 | 42% | $  3 |
| 2004 | $1,027 | $  493 | 48% | $  5 |
| 2005 | $1,295 | $  691 | 53% | $  7 |
| 2006 | $1,537 | $  851 | 55% | $  9 |
| 2007 | $1,925 | $1,070 | 56% | $11 |
| 2008 | $1,797 | $  970 | 54% | $10 |
| 2009 | $1,506 | $  652 | 43% | $  7 |
| 2010 | $1,624 | $  559 | 34% | $  6 |
| Total | | | | **$61** |

*Source: BarclayHedge
**Assumes no incentive fees, as many funds were still below their high water marks following 2008.

FOFs have lost market share in recent years and may have to adopt a different, lower-cost business model, such as providing consulting services. Nonetheless, while the big fees have clearly been earned by the hedge fund managers themselves, FOF managers (who are far fewer in number than hedge fund managers) fully participated in the industry's growth until quite recently. Adding together fees charged by hedge funds and fees charged by funds of hedge funds reveals the figures in Table 4.4: Fees of $379 billion charged by hedge funds and an additional $61BN charged by funds of funds. I calculated Real Investor Profits as $70BN earlier on, but this was before deducting funds of funds fees (hedge fund fees had already been taken out). This may sound complicated—hedge fund returns are calculated net of hedge fund fees, so we know that set of fees has already been deducted. I estimated Funds of Funds fees based on the amount of assets they're managing. For those investors using FOFs they're paying fees on top of fees, so FOF fees have to be deducted from Real Investor Profits to see what's

**Table 4.4**  Everybody's Fees

| Year | Average HF AUM* (BNs) | Real Investor Profits (BNs) | Estimated HF Fees (BNs)** | Estimated FOF Fees (BNs) | Total Fees | Net Real Investor Profits (BNs) | Industry Share of Total Profits |
|------|------|------|------|------|------|------|------|
| 1998 | $ 131 | $ 10 | $ 7 | $ 1 | $ 7 | $ 10 | 44% |
| 1999 | $ 166 | $ 36 | $ 14 | $ 1 | $ 15 | $ 35 | 30% |
| 2000 | $ 213 | $ 17 | $ 12 | $ 1 | $ 13 | $ 16 | 44% |
| 2001 | $ 279 | $ 13 | $ 12 | $ 1 | $ 13 | $ 12 | 52% |
| 2002 | $ 414 | $ 12 | $ 13 | $ 2 | $ 15 | $ 11 | 58% |
| 2003 | $ 666 | $ 82 | $ 36 | $ 3 | $ 38 | $ 79 | 33% |
| 2004 | $1,027 | $ 14 | $ 27 | $ 5 | $ 32 | $ 9 | 78% |
| 2005 | $1,295 | -$ 6 | $ 35 | $ 7 | $ 42 | -$ 13 | 143% |
| 2006 | $1,537 | $ 67 | $ 66 | $ 9 | $ 75 | $ 58 | 56% |
| 2007 | $1,925 | -$ 11 | $ 59 | $11 | $ 70 | -$ 21 | 144% |
| 2008 | $1,797 | -$448 | $ 36 | $10 | $ 46 | -$458 | NM |
| 2009 | $1,506 | $200 | $ 30 | $ 7 | $ 37 | $193 | 16% |
| 2010 | $1,624 | $ 83 | $ 32 | $ 6 | $ 38 | $ 77 | 33% |
| **Total** | | $ 70 | $379 | $61 | $440 | $ 9 | 98% |

*SOURCE: BarclayHedge
**Assumes no incentive fees, as many funds were still below their high water marks following 2008.

actually left, This is the Net Real Investor Profits column. After paying
these fees as well, investors are left with $9BN. Between hedge funds
and funds of funds investors have been charged $440BN, eating up 98
percent of whatever profits have been made.

Even this doesn't fully capture the cost/benefit tradeoff. Many U.S.
institutional investors rely on consultants to advise them on their hedge
fund portfolios. Consultants typically don't have a fiduciary relationship
with their clients, but they do provide specialized knowledge, both on
the industry and on many of the larger managers. For most institutions,
use of a consultant provides a convenient legal liability shield for the
investment committee if things go wrong, in that they can point to an
independent third party's recommendations when explaining investment results to their sponsor. There's no easy way to estimate aggregate
consulting fees—they range from as little as 0.05 percent of assets to as
much as 1 percent. But the numbers as presented here offer a sufficiently
clear story, and in all likelihood they understate the ultimate costs paid
by investors (and therefore overstate the net profits earned by those
same investors).

All the figures in Table 4.4 use the HFRX, an asset-weighted index.
This index was chosen because the purpose is to calculate aggregate
investor returns, so an index that reflects the relative size of hedge funds
is arguably most appropriate. It's also a investable index, meaning that
it is possible to earn its return should an investor be so inclined.
However, the story is substantially the same using the HFRI Global
Index as shown in Table 4.5. Any way you cut it, hedge funds have
been a fabulous business and a lousy investment.

**Table 4.5**  Comparing Different Indices 1998 to 2010

| Index | Real Investor Profits (BNs) | Estimated HF Fees (BNs) | Estimated FOF Fees (BNs) | Total Fees | Net Real Investor Profits (BNs) | Industry Share of Total Profits |
|---|---|---|---|---|---|---|
| **HFRX** | $ 70 | $379 | $61 | $440 | $ 9 | 98% |
| **HFRI Global** | $139 | $418 | $61 | $479 | $78 | 86% |

The hedge fund industry is global, so this isn't simply a case of Wall Street keeping more of the spoils, although the United States and United Kingdom represent a substantial chunk of the industry. Nevertheless, what investors have paid compared with what they've received is almost breathtaking. Hedge fund managers, advisers, consultants, and funds of hedge funds have succeeded in generating substantial profits. However, they've also managed to keep most of these gains for themselves, while at the same time successfully propagating the notion that broad, diversified hedge fund allocations are a smart addition to most institutional portfolios. That's quite a trick!

## Drilling Down by Strategy

The hedge fund industry breaks down into separate strategies, such as long/short equity, relative value, distressed debt, global macro, and so on. Using AUM figures for each strategy, it's possible to estimate which have provided the most egregious mix of fees and (non) performance for investors. Remember, all this analysis is being done using publicly available data. It's just that it has rarely, if ever, been done this way. Hedge fund industry advocates have chosen to focus simply on annual average returns, without looking at gross profits or how those profits are split between clients and the industry.

So using the same technique, while drilling down to the strategy level, reveals the following numbers shown in Table 4.6 for convertible arbitrage. The AUM figures on convertible arbitrage funds are from BarclayHedge, and the returns are from the HFRI Convertible Arbitrage Index. All figures, apart from annual returns, are expressed in billions of dollars.

Hedge funds specializing in convertible arbitrage have earned more than $10 billion in fees since 1998. This figure is the low end of the likely range, for the same reasons as the industry-level figures shown in Table 4.1; it treats the industry like one big hedge fund. Therefore in a year when returns are positive it assumes the industry charged a 20 percent incentive fee, whereas in reality the profitable funds charged a fee, but the unprofitable funds didn't provide an incentive fee rebate.

**Table 4.6** Convertible Arbitrage Hedge Funds Fees and Profits, 1998 to 2010

| Year | Avg AUM* (BNs) | HF Returns | Real Investor Profits (BNs) | Est Total Fees (BNs)** | Fees as % of AUM | Total Profits | Industry Share of Total Profits |
|------|------|------|------|------|------|------|------|
| 1998 | $ 6 | 4% | -$ 0.1 | $ 0.2 | 3% | $ 0.1 | 145% |
| 1999 | $ 6 | 8% | $ 0.2 | $ 0.3 | 4% | $ 0.5 | 54% |
| 2000 | $ 8 | 12% | $ 0.5 | $ 0.4 | 5% | $ 0.9 | 46% |
| 2001 | $13 | 14% | $ 1.3 | $ 0.7 | 5% | $ 2.0 | 35% |
| 2002 | $20 | 12% | $ 1.9 | $ 1.0 | 5% | $ 2.9 | 33% |
| 2003 | $37 | 9% | $ 2.9 | $ 1.6 | 4% | $ 4.5 | 35% |
| 2004 | $54 | 0% | -$ 0.8 | $ 1.1 | 2% | $ 0.3 | 367% |
| 2005 | $47 | −6% | -$ 4.2 | $ 0.9 | 2% | -$ 3.2 | NM |
| 2006 | $36 | 10% | $ 1.7 | $ 1.6 | 4% | $ 3.2 | 49% |
| 2007 | $36 | −1% | -$ 2.1 | $ 0.7 | 2% | -$ 1.4 | NM |
| 2008 | $32 | −58% | -$19.3 | $ 0.6 | 2% | -$18.7 | NM |
| 2009 | $31 | 42% | $12.8 | $ 0.6 | 2% | $13.4 | 5% |
| 2010 | $34 | 9% | $ 3.0 | $ 0.7 | 2% | $ 3.7 | 19% |
| Total | | | -$ 2.1 | $10.4 | | $ 8.3 | 126% |

*SOURCE: BarclayHedge
**Assumes 2 & 20 with no incentive fees after 2008 since so many funds were below their high water mark

Accordingly, in any given year, incentive fees are likely to be more than 20 percent of profits, depending on the mix of winners and losers.[1] And in 2009 and 2010, we've assumed no incentive fees at all across all convertible arbitrage funds, following the disastrous results of 2008, since most managers were below their high water marks. In reality though, it's likely that incentive fees were above 0. Any new inflows after 2008 were probably subject to incentive fees.

[1] To illustrate with a simple example: suppose an investor has two hedge funds, one of which earns $5 million in profit while the other loses $2 million. The profitable hedge fund will charge an incentive fee of $1 million ($5 million × 20 percent) while the losing fund will not charge one. In this way, gross profits of $3 million ($5 million − $2 million) will generate an effective incentive fee of 33 percent ($1 million fee divided by $3 million profit). The investor's net profit will be $2 million.

**Table 4.7**   Distressed Debt Hedge Funds Fees and Profits, 1998 to 2010

| Year | Avg AUM* (BNs) | HF Returns | Real Investor Profits (BNs) | Est Total Fees (BNs)** | Fees as % of AUM | Total Profits | Industry Share of Total Profits |
|------|------|------|------|------|------|------|------|
| 1998 | $   3 | 5% | $  0.0 | $  0.1 | 3% | $  0.1 | 121% |
| 1999 | $   4 | 17% | $  0.4 | $  0.2 | 6% | $  0.7 | 34% |
| 2000 | $   4 | −2% | −$  0.3 | $  0.1 | 2% | −$  0.2 | NM |
| 2001 | $   7 | 21% | $  1.2 | $  0.5 | 7% | $  1.8 | 30% |
| 2002 | $  17 | 10% | $  1.4 | $  0.8 | 4% | $  2.2 | 36% |
| 2003 | $  37 | 21% | $  7.4 | $  2.7 | 7% | $10.1 | 27% |
| 2004 | $  61 | 9% | $  4.7 | $  2.6 | 4% | $  7.3 | 36% |
| 2005 | $  76 | 1% | −$  1.5 | $  1.7 | 2% | $  0.3 | 673% |
| 2006 | $  90 | 10% | $  4.2 | $  4.0 | 4% | $  8.2 | 49% |
| 2007 | $134 | 4% | −$  1.0 | $  4.0 | 3% | $  3.0 | 135% |
| 2008 | $135 | −31% | −$43.6 | $  2.7 | 2% | −$40.9 | NM |
| 2009 | $119 | −6% | −$  6.8 | $  2.4 | 2% | −$  4.5 | NM |
| 2010 | $125 | 8% | $10.2 | $  2.5 | 2% | $12.7 | 20% |
| Total |  |  | −$23.6 | $24.3 |  | $  0.7 | 3622% |

*Source: BarclayHedge
**Assumes 2 & 20 with no incentive fees after 2008 since so many funds were below their high water mark

Compared with the $10.4 billion in fees earned by convertible arbitrage funds, investors actually lost $2.1 billion. They did worse than Treasury bills, while paying a substantial amount for the privilege. As with many things, the 2007 to 2008 credit crisis significantly impacted results, but even up until 2006 the split was: $7.7 billion in fees versus $3.6 billion in Real Investor Profits. In normal times, convertible arbitrage funds and their clients had settled on a roughly 70:30 split in favor of the managers.

Distressed debt provides a similar story as shown in Table 4.7—Real Investor Profits, what investors have earned in excess of riskless Treasury bills, are solidly negative.

Next time you find yourself in a social setting with anybody from the hedge fund industry, you can entertain yourself and others by asking this simple question: **Name a hedge fund client who has made a substantial amount of money by being a hedge fund investor.** Note the word *client* is key here and the question deliberately excludes hedge fund managers themselves, managers of funds of hedge funds, consultants, or anyone who's in the business of making a living from fees charged on hedge fund investments. We're looking for pure investor clients. I started playing this game recently at gatherings of hedge fund professionals, and I can tell you the responses are quite amusing. Once people understand that George Soros isn't an acceptable answer, they stare quizzically at the ceiling while racking their brains for someone, anyone, who's come out ahead. At times I've felt embarrassed, as if I'm asking someone to name the President of the United States and they've drawn a momentary blank. It shouldn't be much more difficult—after all, there are plenty of clients and some of them must have done well. And of course there are successful hedge fund investors, but the trouble so many industry professionals have with this innocuous question and their evident discomfort as they struggle to come up with names reveals more of the inconvenient truth about the hedge fund business than many would like.

Hedge fund managers are rational businesspeople, as well as often being talented investors. As in any free market economy, the provider of a service will seek to maximize his profits in part by raising prices, until competition and sagging demand indicate resistance. In the case of hedge fund managers, the "price" is really the split of total trading profits that investors require in order to remain as clients. The split of profits has been steadily shifting in favor of the hedge fund industry, because investors have broadly accepted steadily worsening terms. Fees charged are high by almost any reasonable standard, but willing buyers (clients) and sellers (hedge fund managers, funds of hedge funds, and consultants) continue to do business at prevailing rates. If consumers continue to pay higher prices for something, it's hard to blame the retailers, who are simply meeting that need. However, in this case the consumers are sophisticated institutional investors and one might think they'd be pressing for more equitable terms.

There are numerous academic articles on the hedge fund industry covering a wide range of topics. Papers have been written on whether hedge funds truly deliver *alpha* (in layman's terms, do they really make money once you properly account for the risk they take); on whether small, new hedge funds do better than older, established ones (they generally do); and on the impact fees have on managers' behavior. One common problem for investors occurs when a small fund enjoys strong success from a strategy that can only absorb a limited amount of capital. New clients flock to the high-performing fund, and eventually the increased level of AUM overwhelms the liquidity in that particular market, making it hard to generate the higher returns of the past.

"Is Pay for Performance effective? Evidence from the Hedge Fund Industry" is a research paper originally published in 2007 (updated in March, 2011) by Bing Ling and Christopher Schwarz, (you can find it at http://ssrn.com/abstract=1333230) which examines this issue systematically. The typical 20 percent incentive fee is supposed to ensure the manager is focused on generating consistently strong performance. In passing, the authors compare the pay-for-performance link managers enjoy with corporate executives. Senior managers of U.S. corporations are often described as overcompensated, relative to the value they create for shareholders. However, they are in the minor leagues compared with hedge fund managers; for a given amount of wealth created for shareholders (or in this case hedge fund investors) hedge fund managers retain around 30 times the share that corporate executives earn! Who would have thought CEOs were so underpaid?

Ling and Schwartz go on to examine whether hedge funds stop taking clients (in industry parlance, they "close" to new money) when they have reached whatever capacity limits their strategy faces. One might think that the incentive fee would be a powerful reason to do just that, since lower returns generate lower incentive fees. But in fact, the data shows otherwise. Many managers reach capacity some time before closing to new money, and in addition, once they've closed their returns are usually not as good as in the past. It's as if the strong commercial instincts of many managers trump maximizing overall returns. But the authors go on to find that managers who allow their AUM to grow too big are still acting rationally, (i.e., maximizing their own profits) because they're able to charge incentive fees on an even bigger pool of capital. If AUM grows faster than returns fall, the manager is still ahead of the game.

Table 4.8 illustrates a simple case. At $1BN in AUM the strategy generated a respectable 10 percent return. At $2BN returns fell to 7 percent, but even though the incentive fee dropped, the greater AUM resulted in higher overall fees.

**Table 4.8**  Why Some Hedge Funds Grow Too Big

|  | Right Amount of AUM | Too Much AUM |
|---|---|---|
| **AUM** | $1BN | $2BN |
| **Returns** | 10% | 7% |
| **Incentive Fee at 20%** | 2% | 1.4% |
| **Incentive Fee** | **$20MM** | **$28MM** |

This example of course doesn't include the 1 to 2 percent management fee which, to the extent it's not all used to run the business, adds to the manager's personal profitability. The paper concludes with the dry observation that "hedge fund managers have a profit maximization function consistent with hoarding assets." In other words, their interests are ultimately best served by growing their business as large as they can, though few managers ever admit that.

## How to Become Richer Than Your Clients

It can be interesting to look at individual hedge funds and see how they did. BarclayHedge maintains an extensive database on returns and AUM for a subset of the hedge fund industry, and from this it's possible to go fund by fund. III (Triple I, originally known as Illinois Income Investors) is one of the oldest hedge funds around. It has a continuous track record that dates back to 1993. It is a fixed-income relative-value fund, which means it trades mortgage-backed securities, interest rate swaps, and other related instruments. They are "picking up pennies in front of the steamroller," in industry parlance, which is to say they identify minor pricing discrepancies and then exploit them profitably through the use of leverage.

I remember meeting one of the principals, Warren Mosler, sometime in the 1990s. Warren struck me as very smart if somewhat eccentric. He was pursuing a hobby of building super-fast sports cars with some of his growing wealth. He seemed somewhat bored with the business, commenting that every year his W-2 was doubling in a way that suggested the whole business was failing to challenge him. Warren

**Table 4.9**   Why Hedge Funds Are Such a Great Business

| | Results from July 1993 to the end of | | |
| --- | --- | --- | --- |
| | **2006** | **2008** | **2010** |
| Average Annual Return | 10.2% | 4.9% | 6.9% |
| Lifetime Investor Profits ($MMs) | 775 | 78 | 160 |
| Lifetime Fees ($MMs) | 441 | 530 | 538 |
| Clients' Share of Profits★ | 64% | 13% | 23% |

★Since client profits are net of fees, adding fees back to client profits results in total profits. So through 2006 for example, total profits were $775 + $441 = $1,216. The clients kept 775/1,216, or 64 percent.
SOURCE: BarclayHedge

had a curious theory of money's role in an economy, which I found hard to follow, but he asserted that the government's role in imposing taxes was a necessary requirement for money to have any actual value (since citizens needed it to pay taxes) and that if the government didn't tax, money would lose its value. For a while afterward he sent me research papers on the topic, though I must say I never fully grasped his insight. III had a spectacular office in West Palm Beach, Florida, facing out over the Atlantic Ocean. It was an idyllic setting and an enviable lifestyle. III went on to many years of success which continues today.

Using the available data, it's possible to estimate investor profits and fees generated over quite a long period of time. These figures are estimates based on AUM and returns. The actual profits earned by III and its clients are private. Table 4.9 is illustrative.

Over 14 years, from 1993 to 2006, III generated an average annual return of 10 percent, producing more than three quarters of a billion dollars in cumulative investor profits. They still managed to haul in more than $400 million in fees for themselves, resulting in clients keeping just less than two thirds of the total profits generated. Because III had grown so large, by the end of 2008 following the worst of the credit crisis, virtually all the profits clients had ever earned from III were gone, although by then the managers had taken their winnings to more than half a billion dollars. As markets recovered, investors made back some of their money, but the end result is still that for one of the longest-lived hedge funds that has delivered generally steady results for

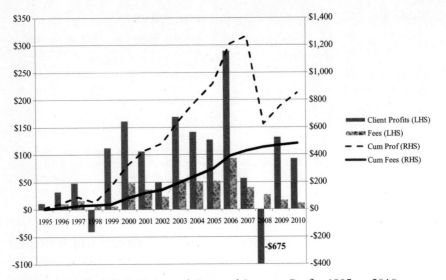

**Figure 4.1**   Stark L.P. Estimated Fees and Investor Profits 1995 to 2010
SOURCE:  BarclayHedge

nearly two decades, the clients have kept less than a quarter of the
trading profits generated. This analysis only covers one of III's funds;
they have others. The results are similar, and the principals have become
very wealthy. The interesting question is whether the wealth created
by the owners has been earned by adding commensurate value to their
clients, or did a set of industry investors hand over substantial sums
while receiving very little in return.

Stark Investments is another old hedge fund that presents a similar
story. From 1995 to 2007 (see Figure 4.1), using the same calculation
assumptions as for III, Stark earned $428 million in fees while its clients
earned $1.26 billion. Stark's managers retained 25 percent of the total
trading results while their clients kept 75 percent. In 2008 trading losses
wiped out half of all the profits the clients had ever earned, and perhaps
not surprisingly Stark's business began to shrink. By 2010 Stark's cumulative fees had reached $480 million and the clients had netted $848
million. This was a better split with clients than for III, but still not
great. If the clients' money had been invested in Treasury bills throughout this entire period they would have earned $490 million. Stark added
$358 million in additional value which works out to be less than 2.5

percent per annum over the risk-free rate and they earned nearly half a billion dollars in the process.

As with all hedge funds, the fees kept growing (the dashed line) even when the results turned down. The contrast between client success and what they paid for it is, well, stark.

## Summary

Sir Winston Churchill, Britain's inspiring leader during World War II, gave many stirring speeches and provided the English language with numerous memorable quotes. In 2002 the BBC broadcast a documentary called "100 Greatest Britons," and by popular vote Churchill was named the Greatest Briton (even ahead of David Beckham). Following the end of the Battle of Britain in 1940 when the Royal Air Force held off the German Luftwaffe in the skies over southern Britain scuttling Hitler's planned invasion, Churchill praised his gallant fighter pilots with the words, "Never in the field of human conflict was so much owed by so many to so few."

Presented with today's hedge fund business, Churchill might comment that, "Never in the history of Finance was so much charged by so many for so little."

There are and always will be some fantastically talented hedge fund managers. Sadly though, for the industry as a whole, it appears that their investment acumen is not as keen as their commercial instincts. The investors who have made this possible owe it to the pension fund beneficiaries and other hapless providers of capital to improve their outcomes.

# Chapter 5

# 2008—The Year Hedge Funds Broke Their Promise to Investors

The events of 2008 will be burnished in the collective memories of investors probably for the rest of our lives. I began my career in 1980 at the London Stock Exchange before moving to New York in 1982. In 1987 I was trading interest rate derivatives for Manufacturers Hanover Trust (a name long forgotten as it's now part of JPMorgan). Trading on Monday, October 19 and in subsequent days is an experience I'll never forget. All the mathematical links that connected the prices of securities, futures, and swaps were stretched beyond all recognition. We watched with morbid fascination that day as stock prices sank and then collapsed, wiping out more than 20 percent of the market's value in just a few hours. Slowly at first but then with increasing speed, bond prices reversed their decline as the bear market abruptly ended. A rising trade deficit and depreciating U.S. dollar had been driving down Treasury bond prices for months, but the economy had remained strong and stock prices had been rising most of the year. The new Fed chairman Alan Greenspan had begun raising rates that Summer to establish his inflation fighting credentials in following inflation's conqueror Paul Volcker. The falling U.S. dollar, falling bonds, and rising stocks—the markets had been feeding off one another in a familiar dance.

During the late afternoon of that extraordinary Monday and into the Tokyo session that night, bond prices began to rise (i.e., interest rates began falling) as the markets contemplated an economic slowdown or even a recession induced by the sudden loss of wealth caused by the stock market crash. Incidentally, that evening following the 508 point drop in the Dow Jones Industrial Average, I solemnly warned my wife that we should start accumulating stores of canned food in preparation for the coming Depression. Television footage of soup lines from the 1930s that followed the 1929 stock market crash were already playing on the nightly news. History was surely going to repeat. My wife, who was grounded in the real world and was thankfully not of Wall Street, breezily replied that regardless of what had happened on Wall Street, Main Street didn't care. Life would not change, she asserted. It was simply a problem for "you traders." I dismissed her naiveté. The tidal wave was coming to Main Street; it had simply hit Wall Street first. But of course she was right, and gross domestic product (GDP) growth barely stumbled in the months ahead.

## Financial Crisis, 1987 Version

For fixed income traders such as me, the following day Tuesday, October 20 was more memorable than the 19th as the sharp turn in bond sentiment translated into breathtaking volatility. At the time I traded Eurodollar futures and interest rate swaps, similar instruments that provided opportunities to arbitrage between the two of them. My trading partner and I arrived at work early that Tuesday morning intending to develop a plan, but the phone lines from brokers were all flashing urgently with trades to be done so we just plunged in and started trading. It seemed as if the whole world needed to buy Treasury bonds and Eurodollar futures, anything that would pay a reliable interest rate. One of my clearest memories is doing a trade that required me to buy Eurodollar futures as a hedge.

Why did I short the market when it seemed as if everybody was already short? We were market makers and I traded with a trader at another bank at a price that reflected utter panic-stricken urgency on his part. I had built in almost 2 percent of cushion on the trade, an enormous spread since at that time arbitrage margins on those types of trade were typically 0.1 percent (10 basis points, or about one twentieth of the spread I'd priced in on this trade). So I called up our broker on the London futures exchange (it was early; U.S. exchanges were not yet open) and following futures prices on the screen while I dialed I watched my expected profit rapidly melt away. Incredibly, the London broker reported "no offers" as he screamed across the exchange floor. Rather than bid into a one-sided market (i.e., one with no offers) I resolved to wait a few minutes until the CME (Chicago Mercantile Exchange) opened the far larger U.S. Eurodollar futures market. I watched with fascinated horror as the March 1988 futures contract, which represented three-month Libor in only five months' time, rose in price from its close the previous day of 89.20 to trade at 94.00. I can still remember the numbers to this day; it was such a blistering experience. The market went from expecting Libor in March to be 10.8 percent on one day to expecting it to be only 6 percent less than a day later. As my highly profitable trade swung to a large loss, I tried to contemplate just how bad it could get. How much could I lose on what was a relatively small trade? I paused for a few moments, thinking, looking for some firm guideposts that would show where futures "ought" to be. There was nothing; the market had no anchors, nothing was tethered to anything else, bond and futures prices could go anywhere they wanted. The familiar mathematical relationships were shredded. Everything was pure emotion. The bond market was at that time on that day simply a poker game separating the weak hands from their money, handing it to the emotionally stronger.

I waited. Following a buying frenzy futures fell a dizzying 100 points (i.e., a 1 percent jump in interest rates) in about 10 minutes as the buyers briefly vanished. I gratefully covered at a small loss and moved on. There was so much activity, so many trading opportunities, and no time to dwell on that first trade. We plunged in, buying low, selling high, exploiting the market dislocations as we reacted to prices on screens and from brokers with mostly mental arithmetic. There just wasn't time to input numbers into a computer; they moved too sharply, the result was out of date before the enter key was pressed. Some trades were winners and some were losers, but we kept moving. Doing our type of trading in that market was like playing in the F.A. Cup Final (English football's rough equivalent to the Super Bowl) except that we'd arrived there without warning. This was our moment—don't think more than two minutes ahead, just react to the ball.

By the end of the day as we totaled everything up, my partner and I had made a record daily trading profit for our desk. The numbers were laughably small by comparison with today's trading profits, but we were exhausted and exhilarated. We knew we'd experienced history and a supreme test of our abilities. We were amongst the winners. We were young, and youth can be wonderfully intoxicating in a trader; trading losses rarely hurt, because youthful confidence allows breezy self-forgiveness and a belief that next time will be better. As I got older I became less tolerant of the pain of losing money and less willing to expose myself to financial harm. But those few days in 1987 are permanently burnt in my memory, from a time very early in my trading career. Incidentally, my trading partner back then was Barry Wittlin. Barry is one of the most gifted interest rate traders I've ever known. A few years later he joined Merrill Lynch before setting up his own hedge fund in 2007. Barry doesn't seek the spotlight but is a true intellectual giant, and I have no doubt he is in the process of using his prodigious talent to build himself a fortune and make his wealthy clients wealthier.

## How 2008 Redefined Risk

For 20 years following the 1987 Crash I was confident that the world would never experience something quite like that again. Looking back today, no doubt we all wish that our problems had simply been caused by an overreliance on portfolio insurance whose subsequent effects on the economy were quite fleeting. But the credit crisis of 2007 and 2008 was of a completely different order of magnitude. It exposed gaping holes in regulation, widespread lapses in judgment, and risk-management failures across huge swathes of finance. Its effects are of course still with us today in the form of unsustainable levels of government debt and (in the United States) stubbornly high unemployment. And much as we'd like to think that the crash to end all crashes has resulted in regulatory and systemic changes to ensure it will never repeat, the biggest change has been to investor risk appetites. The regulatory framework has tightened but not in ways that meaningfully address the causes. Big banks are still too big to fail, and so enjoy an implicit government guarantee. Capital standards are still too light on banks that trade for themselves and underwrite securities. The result is that the split of profits in banking between the providers of capital (investors) and labor (management and revenue producers) is too favorable to the latter. Requiring higher capital of the largest banks that do enjoy an implicit government guarantee would redress the imbalance. If bigger really is better in banking as some have argued, then bigger banks should be able to generate higher returns on capital and so cover the cost of maintaining even stronger balance sheets.

A number of fine books have been written on the credit crisis. Roger Lowenstein (*The End of Wall Street*), Michael Lewis (*The Big Short*), Andrew Ross Sorkin (*Too Big to Fail*), Gregory Zuckerman (*The Greatest Trade Ever*), and former Treasury Secretary Hank Paulson (*On the Brink*) cover the territory thoroughly and I won't repeat here well-known episodes that have already been chronicled. John Paulson's spectacular trade that profited from his early identification of the real estate bubble is accurately named in the title to Greg Zuckerman's book, and surely every investment professional can only marvel at the insight and execution Paulson demonstrated at that time.

But as fantastic as Paulson's, and a few others, results were, in general hedge fund returns in 2008 were of course breathtakingly poor. Losses were way beyond any reasonable expectations, as was in many cases the reaction of managers to the existential threats their businesses faced as a result. The hedge fund industry lost 19 to 23 percent for investors, depending on which return series you're looking at and was truly awful by any measure. What made it even worse was that this result occurred after a period of unprecedented growth in the industry.

Investors had been flocking to hedge funds as discussed in Chapter 1, and assets under management (AUM) had grown from $118 billion in 1997 to $2.1 trillion by the end of 2007, an 18-fold leap in only 10 years! A small percentage of the assets managed by the hedge fund industry had been around to enjoy the strong years of the late 1990s and 2003, and so 2008 was devastating to the aggregate results. In fact, in losing between $400 and $500 billion in 2008 the industry essentially wiped out all of the collective profits that investors had earned over the prior 10 years. Given how small the industry was before that, it's probably safe to say that 2008 destroyed all the value that hedge funds had ever created. This does not mean of course that nobody had made any money in hedge funds, simply that the total of all the money made and lost by all the investors was, unfortunately, negative.

Whenever I interviewed hedge fund managers as part of our due diligence, I would routinely ask them how much we could expect to lose in a bad year. Risk is described in many ways. Back in the 1990s managers used to say they were striving for "equity-like returns with bond-like volatility" when equities were doing well. Others might describe their objectives as to outperform their peer group on a risk-adjusted basis, or even volunteer a specific return target range (say, 8 to 12 percent). None of these are necessarily bad answers, and asking open-ended questions can often elicit a greater understanding of the manager's parameters. But ultimately risk is about how much you can lose, and the question was typically something like, "How much should I be prepared to lose on my investment before concluding that I should revisit my original decision to invest with you." I haven't asked this question since 2008 because I haven't invested in a new hedge fund manager, and I imagine today's answers might be different. However, a 10 percent loss was a remarkably common response to this question, with a 15 percent loss being the absolute worst case anyone should expect. That was then of course, and few of us thought equities could lose 37 percent in a single year either, which was the enormous miti-gating factor for every investment manager in 2008. Nonetheless, hedge funds were long thought of as absolute return vehicles with results that are uncorrelated with traditional assets. The year when your equity investments are down 37 percent is precisely the year when you want your absolute return investments to look least like the rest of your portfolio, and hedge funds in general showed that in extreme times they have many of the same risks as traditional assets.

2008 also exposed some critical weaknesses in the way investors access hedge funds, normally through commingled vehicles, either limited partnership [LP] structures or offshore corporations in banking centers such as the Grand Cayman Islands. As discussed in Chapter 7, the LP structure provides significant business model benefits for the manager that are generally to the disadvantage of clients. By putting all the clients into one fund and then treating that fund as in effect one big client, the operational aspects of trading are greatly simplified. It also allows the manager to withhold detailed information about what positions he's actually holding, making it harder for the investor to analyze results and determine whether they're as good as they should be given the risks involved. Managers can use the LP structure to avoid negotiating concessions (on fees, for example) to investors by arguing that all the LPs in a given fund have to be treated equally. Nonetheless, sideletters are often used to define special rights an investor has that are not afforded to all the other investors, and so some investors then incorporate "most favored nation" clauses. This is a catch-all that basically says, ". . . if you give somebody else a better deal than mine you have to come back and give it to me too." But at the end of the day investors are dealing with the manager bilaterally, and can rarely act in concert with one another.

## The Hedge Fund as Hotel California

The ability of investors to withdraw their money from a hedge fund varies widely depending on the liquidity of the underlying strategy and the strength of demand a manager assesses amongst his clients. Really, redemptions should only be affected by liquidity, but stable capital makes for a stable business. Permanent capital, with no possibility of withdrawal, is every large manager's ultimate goal. The security of knowing that investors cannot flee at the worst time, forcing the manager to possibly dump securities at fire sale prices, can provide access to highly illiquid but deeply underpriced investments and certainly has its place. However, capital generally likes to know it can be moved if needed, and the open-ended fund structure that is widely prevalent has met the needs of managers while being accepted by investors. 2008 threw up numerous examples of the impediments to liquidity that were not all the result of dysfunctional markets. Just as in the song by the Eagles, some investors found that they could check out but never leave.

*Gate* is a term applied to restrictions a manager can impose on investors trying to withdraw money. Generally speaking, a gate allows a manager to suspend redemptions if too many investors are trying to withdraw capital at the same time, which might require the manager to raise more cash than markets will easily allow. A fund might restrict more than, say, 10 percent of its capital from leaving at once, or may temporarily suspend redemptions during an unusual and temporary loss of market liquidity. Used properly, they're a legitimate feature of the normal hedge fund structure. In fact, it's hard to imagine a hedge fund operating without a gate unless it was in highly liquid instruments such as large-cap developed market equities or futures, for example. Many institutional investors even require such a feature before investing, so as to protect themselves against untimely withdrawals by too many other clients. Indeed, hedge fund investors care who the other clients are. Everybody wants long-term, stable money from people who will not panic during periods of turbulence. But the knowledge that a manager can restrict withdrawals can sometimes induce game theory type behavior from investors. Rather like a run on the bank, if you think others will ask for their cash and there's only limited availability (i.e., the gate may be lowered), you'd better get your request in before others. Sometimes redemptions are met in sequential order, and sometimes all the requests in a given period (month or quarter) are treated equally. This is where you have to read the fine print. And sometimes an investor may put in a "contingent" redemption request, which basically means they may want to rescind it if, for instance, it turns out nobody else is redeeming and they fear not being able to return to what they think in the long run will be a good investment.

In many ways, investors are a large part of the problem. Managers often complain that investors don't fully understand the strategy and so overreact at short-term volatility. Or that investors claim to be "long term" and not overly worried about month-to-month volatility when in fact they are anything but. Although there are plenty of exceptions, to a very large degree hedge funds have stuck to their strategies, followed their agreements, and done what they said. In many cases the disappointing results are as much the fault of investors as anything else. Poor analysis that fails to fully grasp the risks and intricacies of a strategy; momentum investing, chasing high performing managers without sufficient regard for whether the favorable environment for their strategy will persist or not; underestimating the negative impact of increasing AUM size (both for the industry as well as individual managers). These are all reasons why investors as a whole have not done as well as they should have. Hedge funds have responded to demand for a service and charged what the market will bear. But the best hedge fund managers are highly intelligent, and hedge fund managers overall are in my judgment smarter than their clients. Investors need to recognize their intellectual disadvantage and apply more skepticism to their often star-struck postures. As Warren Buffett famously said, if in a game of poker you don't know who the patsy is, you're the patsy!

So by the time 2008 rolled around hedge fund investors had more than $2 trillion invested across a wide range of strategies. This money was allocated in part based on past returns the industry had generated using far less capital, but at least for investors at that time this did not present a problem. Gates and other restrictions on investor withdrawals, concepts often clearly spelled out in documents but rarely dwelled on, all of a sudden became a very real concern. Whether investors needed money to meet other obligations (such as to fund prior commitments to private equity, or to meet their own withdrawals in the case of funds of hedge funds) or simply because they were nervous (and who wasn't scared about the financial system itself at times in 2008?), gates and restrictions on redemptions became very real that year.

Part of the problem stemmed from the fact that managers often have substantial discretion in deciding that market conditions warrant such constraints being used. There's no easy way to derive a legal definition of a dysfunctional market. It's typically subject to the pornography test ("I know it when I see it," as attributed to U.S. Supreme Court Justice Potter Stewart in Jacobellis v. Ohio, 1964). Given the weight of redemptions facing many managers during 2008, meeting them meant the possible failure of their businesses as remaining investors might flee on seeing a precipitous drop in AUM. While inconsistent with the spirit in which such restrictions are supposed to be imposed, at that time who could tell? The line between protecting investors and protecting a business became blurred in many cases, and investors relying on the open-ended fund structure to allow their exit found out the hard way that managers can maintain substantial control over their money.

*AR* magazine reported at the end of 2008 that requests to withdraw more than $100 billion were submitted in the course of that year, and that 10 to 15 percent of total industry assets were being sought (Williamson, 2008). Many large and well-known hedge funds saw fit to place restrictions on their clients' ability to withdraw capital. A partial list (Brewster, 2008), with each fund's AUM in parentheses where available, includes:

- Polygon ($8 billion)
- Grosvenor Capital
- Peloton (Denmark, 2008) ($3 billion), which ultimately closed down
- London Diversified Fund (Mackintosh, "Hedge Funds extend redemption ban," 2008) ($3 billion) which later shrank to less than $500 million
- Atlas Capital ($4.3 billion)
- Fortress ($8 billion) which noted at the time that meeting redemptions would cause it to violate debt covenants and allow banks to call in loans that had extended (Mackintosh, "Hard Hit hedge funds forced to renegotiate banking terms," 2008)
- Farallon (Mackintosh, "Hard hit hedge funds forced to renegotiate banking terms," 2008) ($30 billion)
- Blue Mountain (Bowman, 2008) ($3.1 billion)
- Tudor Investment Corp (Williamson, "Redemption requests Bode Ill," 2008) ($10 billion), run by industry legend Paul Jones

In fact, because some widely respected funds such as Tudor saw the need to suspend redemptions it greatly lessened the stigma associated with such a decision.

A quite staggering episode involved Randy Lerner, billionaire owner of the Cleveland Browns NFL franchise and Aston Villa (an English football club) in 2010. A dispute arose with a hedge fund he had seeded when he tried to withdraw his investment. The manager of the fund, Paige Capital, suspended redemptions because Mr. Lerner's withdrawal represented more than 20 percent of the fund's assets. Although this is not an uncommon mechanism to protect investors that don't wish to redeem, in this case Mr. Lerner represented almost all the assets in the fund. It was in virtually all respects his fund. Nonetheless, the case wound up in court, and as (Vardi, "Billionaire Cleveland Browns Owner Claims Hedge Fund Is Hiding His Money," 2010) memorably quoted from the court documents, "[W]e are fully prepared to litigate this matter to the bitter end because we will continue to manage your money, and collect management and incentive fees, until this matter is resolved many years hence," Christopher Paige, Paige Capital's general counsel, defiantly wrote in a March letter, court filings show. "You cannot win because you will spend more litigating than we're fighting over . . . we decide the best way to protect the funds, and your opinion is irrelevant." This was to say the least an unconventional reaction from a fiduciary.

In August 2011 a court ordered that Lerner's money be returned. (Kaulessar, 2011).

One fund that surprised me personally was the London Diversified Fund. This was run by Rob Standing and Dave Gorton, and was spun out from JPMorgan London's Rates business. I had known Rob for many years, since the merger between Manufacturers Hanover Trust and Chemical Bank in 1992. Rob managed Chemical London's trading business in interest rate derivatives and continued in that role through subsequent mergers with Chase Manhattan and JPMorgan. As I came to know Rob, I developed enormous respect for his intellect and trading ability. He had an uncanny ability to immediately see through an issue and accurately assess how markets would react. He enjoyed enormous admiration amongst his traders in London and led them to consistently higher profits year after year. One of his senior traders, the quietly spoken and thoughtful Ashley Bacon, once said to me simply that, "Rob is always right." Not in the way that Rob always believed he was right (though he was rarely burdened by self-doubt) but that Rob was simply right when it came to assessing how a market or derivatives relationship would react. That was pretty high praise, since I'd found Ashley was usually right too!

Dave Gorton was a highly successful proprietary trader who worked for Rob Standing. Dave was very talented, combining the detailed yield curve analysis that was the hallmark of the entire London trading room with sound judgment about the short-term trends that could provide good entry and exit points for his trades. He took very large positions, so large in fact that the bank had brought in outside capital for him to trade alongside its own. Dave was able to exceed Chase's risk appetite, but his consistent profitability attracted traditional hedge fund investors. Essentially, the London Diversified Fund was born out of Rob Standing and Dave Gorton's ability to generate growing trading profits that outgrew the availability of internal capital.

Although Rob had responsibility to oversee dozens of traders with substantial levels of risk and profit and loss (P&L), he maintained a seat on the trading desk and was most often to be found sitting there trading like everyone else, the ultimate player-coach. By then Rob's trading positions were rarely the largest, but his results were consistently among the most stable in the trading room. Dave Gorton once memorably confessed to me that, "I just look at what positions Rob has on and then do 10 times the size." In that one brief sentence he illustrated his enormous respect for Rob as well as his own almost limitless self confidence.

In 2002 Rob Standing, Dave Gorton, and a handful of others left JPMorgan and set up London Diversified Fund (LDF) as an independent hedge fund. It was a great deal for them financially, since they were able to retain the capital they were managing while at the bank. They continued their steady profitability over subsequent years.

But something went wrong for them during the credit crisis. I recall meeting with Rob in London in late 2006, when markets were strong and there was no apparent sign of looming financial disaster. Rob was very concerned; he felt markets were fragile, and that the regulatory authorities had a very tenuous understanding of the financial system's vulnerability. I must confess the signs weren't nearly as apparent to me, but I listened as Rob quickly articulated his case factually but with judgments blended in. And as is so often the case, he was right. Only this time, unusually and maybe uniquely, his risk positions and P&L didn't reflect his insight. For 13 years prior to 2007 LDF had averaged 12 to 14 percent annual returns, with their worst losing period being

−3.2 percent. In terms of return versus risk, this must have been one of the best track records around. Then in 2008 as the crisis took hold, they dropped 28 percent.

I wasn't in contact with them during this time, but people I spoke to who were described how the traders under Dave's direction had moved away from the generic interest rate derivatives and government debt trading that was for so long their bread and butter, and had begun taking positions in less liquid, more complex securities including mortgages. It was evidently a step too far away from their expertise and the resulting losses were many times greater than any of the investors might have reasonably expected. Of all the hedge funds in the world, I was probably more familiar with LDF's trading style than any other through our shared background in the same trading division at Chemical Bank and Chase in the 1990s. Although I wasn't a client of theirs, I would have felt safer investing with Rob than any other hedge fund manager in the world. Events and people can surprise you. Their business of course shrank, falling from more than $5 billion to less than $500 million. Rob and Dave carved up the capital so as to trade independently of one another, and the page was turned on that chapter.

Incidentally, their marketing guy Mark Corbett saved one of my clients a great deal of money through hubris. Mark was in the right place at the right time; when I first met him he was in an operational role supporting the trading business at Chase London. His was essentially a back office position, involved in the necessary details of accounting and trade settlement that take place in the background but far away from the thought process through which money was made. In time he took on a more public role representing LDF to outside investors, both before the fund was spun out of JPMorgan and afterward. In fact, he became a very able spokesman for the fund and was able to talk credibly with people about the positions they took and their risk controls, even though he'd never held a trading position himself. One investor once commented to me after seeing Mark give a presentation what a talented trader he was, and I wouldn't be surprised if some people thought Mark really was the brains behind the operation.

Part of Mark's role was to jealously protect Rob and Dave's valuable time. Meeting with clients or prospects meant fewer hours spent analyzing the markets. Clients were not allowed to meet with both

Rob and Dave together, and potential clients had to first go through a meeting with Mark to establish that a subsequent follow-up with Rob or Dave was going to be worthwhile. Masters of the Universe can manage their time in this way, and placing the client in the role of supplicant establishes very clearly who has the upper hand in the relationship. My client, the CIO of a large pension fund (we'll call him George, not his real name) wanted to meet Rob and Dave because he was considering an investment. George wasn't based in London but was going to be there on business and wanted to meet the principals. Mark wouldn't allow this departure from his normal role as gatekeeper and screener, so politely refused. I even called Rob and explained George was a very knowledgeable investor who didn't have time to meet their former operations guy first, and although Rob agreed, the next day Mark called me to reassert his control of the castle. He chided me for trying to run around him; there were to be no exceptions.

Fortunately, George had the good sense to know when his time wasn't being respected, and as a result no meetings took place. We should have thanked Mark, he saved at least one investor some money.

Some hedge fund managers tried cutting fees in order to encourage investors to look beyond their immediate needs for cash. While few would describe hedge fund fees as low, if your interest is in retrieving your capital urgently for fear there will be less of it if you delay, reducing the normal 20 percent incentive fee to 15 percent (as Ramius Capital did) (Avery, 2008), which might improve later returns by perhaps 1 percent, scarcely seems as if it should alter the overall risk assessment. It was a nice gesture though. London-based Centaurus Capital offered (Mackintosh, "Record 40 billion is redeemed from poorly performing hedge funds," 2008) to charge 1.5 and 15, a 25 percent cut, and allow investors up to 30 percent of their capital back if they would lock up the remainder for a further 12 months. Camulos Capital similarly offered to cut fees for investors who would agree to remain invested (Taub, 2008). In spite of these and other concessions borne of desperate times, the fee structure for hedge funds in general didn't really change much.

In addition, large numbers of funds closed down following large losses, including Ospraie, Drake Capital, MKM Longboat (Mackintosh, "Hedge fund withdrawal expected by managers," 2008), Peloton, and many others. JWM Partners, John Meriwether's Phoenix-like return after he almost took down the financial system in 1998 with Long Term Capital Management, was down 26 percent (Rose-Smith, 2008) through October 2008. While in life people often deserve a second chance, you have to wonder at the judgment of the investors who went into JWM after Meriwether wiped out the first set of clients. What exactly is the analysis that concludes it's an attractive opportunity, apart from a conviction that lightning doesn't strike twice? Whatever John Meriwether's investment skills, his marketing abilities are clearly stronger.

## Timing and Tragedy

The collapse of Lehman Brothers in September 2008 triggered all kinds of unexpected consequences. Many hedge funds had obtained prime broker financing from Lehman's London subsidiary which allowed them to circumvent Federal Reserve constraints on leverage (known as "Regulation T"). When Lehman filed for bankruptcy protection under Chapter 13 of the U.S. bankruptcy code, its London subsidiary fell under U.K. bankruptcy law, which, as everyone soon learned to their dismay, operates differently and with apparently less urgency than in the United States. Many otherwise-solvent hedge funds with collateral now locked in Lehman International faced very real difficulties in meeting client redemptions. To name just a couple, New York's Bay Harbor Management had $190 million seized (Adamson, 2008) and Harbinger Capital Partners was looking for $250 million. MKM closed down their $1.5 billion multi-strategy fund because of poor performance but also because of their Lehman exposure. In an ironic twist, many hedge funds were forced to restrict client redemptions because they themselves had been restricted in accessing their capital from Lehman. While many of the events were almost impossible to anticipate and may well qualify as the proverbial thousand-year flood, the complexity of the hedge fund structure rendered many of these risks unknowable to investors. I attended meetings that year during which we quizzed managers on their prime broker relationships and Lehman was a concern for some time prior to their failure in September. But few could have been aware of the additional exposure created by a trans–Atlantic bankruptcy straddling two quite different sets of statutes and credit treatment.

One tragic story I followed concerned Marc Cohodes of Copper River. Marc's fund was a short seller, one of only a handful of hedge funds that sought to make most if not all of their money by shorting stocks. Copper River was originally known as Rocker Partners after its founder David Rocker. David was based in New York while Marc was in California. Following David's retirement the name changed to Copper River and Marc assumed full control.

Hedge fund managers that concentrate on running short portfolios are among the most thick-skinned people in the industry. Many hedge funds short stocks, and that in itself is a fraught activity. Significant forces are lined up against you—for a start, the target company's management may vilify you and engage in all kinds of attempts to discredit you and cause the stock price to rise, costing you money. For a case study of how this can happen, go no further than David Einhorn's absorbing story, "Fooling Some of the People All of the Time" in which he recounts his multi-year battle against Allied Capital's fraudulent accounting. David was ultimately proved right, but retaining the conviction of his research required unimaginable fortitude in the face of government indifference and Wall Street opposition. Shorting stocks requires borrowing them for extended periods of time, which requires ensuring their long-term availability. And there's always the possibility of a short squeeze, when speculators may buy the target company's shares in the hope of forcing the short seller to cover his position, driving the price up even higher. The basic math is also adverse, in that an unprofitable position grows while an unprofitable one shrinks (quite the opposite of what happens if you're long). This is because the market value of a position goes up when the stock price rises, and it falls when the stock falls. A basic measure of risk is to look at the size of the position. If a long position doubles in value, it's typically thought of as more risky because a 10% move in the price now has twice the impact. This is just as true if it's a short position—a doubling in price for a short position also doubles the risk. The problem for the short position is that losses can grow quite rapidly if the stock rallies, and at least theoretically there is no limit on how much you can lose. Meanwhile your maximum profit is limited to the price you sold the stock at—it can't go below zero. So shorts assume more risk as they rise in price, meaning that a losing position becomes a bigger one. This is quite the opposite of what happens with a long position, since it becomes bigger only by being profitable. As a result of all this, the research that's required to justify a short position has to be exhaustive. It's a hard way to make money.

But while many hedge funds short stocks, very few limit themselves to *only* shorting stocks. They are a breed apart. Typically they combine the requisite deep research on individual companies with a broader conviction that the entire financial system is at risk, and very dark times lie ahead. Many long/short hedge funds maintain a net long exposure to the market because they believe over time the market rises. They incorporate the higher long-term returns they expect from stocks into their risk profile. Meanwhile, short selling funds have the opposite worldview. They see a great deal wrong with the world, and anticipate financial destruction, depression, mass unemployment, and all manner of terrible outcomes for the global economy and society as a whole.

On top of this, they often believe that the companies they short are riddled with criminal behavior and will ultimately go bankrupt. They expect management to one day be led out of their offices handcuffed and in full view of the TV cameras (the so-called "perp walk") as the ultimate vindication of their detailed research. Most investors will recognize that even the greatest companies can have an overpriced stock, and be willing to separate a well-run business from a poor investment. Short sellers believe the annihilation of their shorted stock is inevitable. The only fair price is $0.

In early 2008 I was at a conference where Marc Cohodes spoke about his investments. His outlook was negative; already cracks were appearing in the mortgage market, and the consequences of America's profligate behavior were about to become devastatingly clear. Marc's entertaining speech then continued to identify specific companies who were vulnerable. He held up a newspaper ad for Jos. A. Bank, the men's clothing retailer. "Buy one suit, get two free" he shouted. "How is this possible?" Marc went on to pick apart the company's business model, noting that they possessed no sought-after patented technology and operated in a fairly mundane, competitive marketplace. How could they possibly survive, undercutting the competition by so much?

Ultimately their cashflow would falter and the whole deck of cards would come tumbling down. Jos. A. Bank surely had to be engaged in some very questionable accounting practices, and like any dodgy scheme its collapse was only a matter of time. Marc was shorting their stock.

2008 should have been a spectacular vindication of Marc Cohodes. The unthinkable, which Marc had been thinking for a long time, very nearly came to pass as the entire financial system teetered on the verge of collapse that September. Every asset was down, except for riskless government bonds. Seemingly, a short position in just about any security would have generated a handsome profit. Marc had been anticipating this for a very long time. Lehman's bankruptcy should have been his crowning glory, and in a year when hedge funds were losing hundreds of billions of dollars for their clients, Copper River should have been the champion, the winner when most were losers, the fund that showed who really deserved the word "hedge" in their description. But things did not turn out that way.

Copper River had put on short positions using Lehman as a counterparty. When Lehman failed on September 15, Copper River wound up like so many other hedge funds, with collateral tied up and at least temporarily inaccessible. On top of that, Lehman then closed out the short positions they had put on to hedge their trades with Copper River, driving up the prices of the stocks Marc was short. Then on September 19, the Securities and Exchange Commission (SEC) issued unprecedented restrictions on short sales of a number of companies including banks, which caught the market off guard and caused a sharp rally in the prices of many financial stocks. Copper River reported to investors that over two weeks they had lost 55 percent of their clients' capital (Boyd, 2008). Within months the business was closed down in the face of heavy redemptions. Almost everybody had a bad year in 2008, but one can scarcely imagine the abject frustration Marc felt as he contemplated the gulf between his views and the financial results he had to show for it. Few people deserve sympathy for that year, but Marc may be among the small minority that merits consideration.

Almost every day I walk past the local Jos. A. Banks store. They're still offering incredible deals on men's suits, and their stock made a new all time high in 2011. I don't know how they do it, but it seems they still do. The story of Marc Cohodes is as close to a tragedy as you'll find in the hedge fund industry.

## In 2008, Down Was a Long Way

Observers worried quite naturally about the very survival of the hedge fund industry. Daniel Celeghin, a director with Casey, Quirk & Associates, commented "The key question right now is: Does the hedge fund industry survive in its current form?" He went on to add, "If it does not survive, it will be because financing has changed drastically." (Rose-Smith, "Goodbye, easy money," 2008) Meaning that both the terms under which hedge funds borrowed but also the terms investors faced as clients were destined to change to reflect the new reality. Marc Freed of Lyster Watson (a hedge fund investor) noted that as much as $400 billion was locked up and added "There are more assets frozen in suspended hedge funds than the $325 billion distributed to date under the Tarp (Sender, 2008)." Subsequent data from BarclayHedge suggests that about $180 billion was withdrawn in 2008 as the industry shrank from $2.1 trillion in AUM to $1.5 trillion (negative performance accounted for the balance of the shrinkage in AUM), and a further $100 billion was withdrawn in 2009.

As the year wore on, observers increasingly feared for the survival of hedge funds in anything like their current form. For example, in October 1988 Mick Gilligan (Johnson, 2008), collectives analyst at Killik & Co, a London-based broker, said: "Whenever we speak to people at hedge fund groups they say they have had large requests and they expect to have large requests to the year end. There is a huge deleveraging process going on. A lot of money went into hedge funds in recent years and a lot of that was safe haven money, and that will be coming out."

As the industry speculated about which funds might be forced to liquidate positions to meet redemptions, attention focused on positions believed to be widely held. Goldman Sachs (and no doubt others) maintained a list of 50 "very important" hedge fund positions and in one research note said that "forced selling to cover redemptions and deleveraging by hedge funds has put downward pressure on selected stocks." (Sender, "Hedge funds exploiting rivals' woes," 2008) Like a group of drowning men struggling to survive, traders were pushing each other underwater in their efforts to stay afloat.

# Summary

2008 was a year that redefined for investors how bad things could really be. Hedge funds were certainly not alone in losing far more for their clients than anybody previously thought possible. Stocks, bonds (other than government bonds), emerging markets, private equity, and of course real estate all delivered thumping losses as the financial system very nearly collapsed.

As the *Wall Street Journal* noted in its review of 2008, some notable hedge funds were forced to close, including Peloton (a London-based fund invested in mortgages) and Ospraie's biggest commodity fund run by Dwight Anderson, while many high profile funds including Citadel and Highbridge Capital Management suffered deep losses. Citigroup had bought fund of hedge funds Old Lane Partners in 2007 with the idea of jumpstarting its hedge fund activities for clients. Co-founder Vikram Pandit negotiated the $800 million sale and joined Citi as a senior executive, ultimately taking over as CEO later that year.

Having generated a no doubt substantial part of his personal net worth through that well-timed sale to Citigroup, Pandit as CEO then oversaw the complete write down of the investment as Old Lane added to the financial giant's losses in 2008. As they say, you just can't make this stuff up.

The hedge fund industry additionally had to deal with the massive fraud of Bernie Madoff, which provided nervous hedge fund investors further reason to worry not just how much money they had left but whether it was really there at all.

However, amidst all the financial destruction were the seeds for recovery, and phoenix-like markets and hedge funds rebounded the following year. For the survivors of 2008, those who had managed to preserve enough capital to be buyers, almost every market offered opportunities rarely seen before. The rebound had begun.

# Chapter 6

# The Unseen Costs
# of Admission

The hedge fund net asset value (NAV) is the price at which investors enter and exit. The fact that it is a single figure (i.e., inflows and outflows occur at the same price even if they don't offset each other, which they rarely do) makes it appear a much more precise measure of value than is often the case. It also takes no account of the costs incurred by a fund whenever new money needs to be invested or capital raised to meet redemptions. In fact the whole subject of transaction costs is one that's rarely visible to the investor. Hedge funds pay enormous amounts of commissions and incur additional market impact costs whenever they cross the bid/ask spread. In many markets, the cost of the bid/ask spread can be substantially more than commissions, but it's not directly observable by the investor.

Consider a hedge fund investing in corporate bonds needing to invest additional capital received from a new investor. The quoted market amongst bond dealers for one of the bonds the hedge fund needs to buy might be 80-81 (i.e., bid at 80, offered at 81). If no motivated sellers are around, the hedge fund would buy the bonds from a dealer at 81, and assuming no actual change in prices, the closing value on those bonds would be 80.5 (mid-way between the bid and offer). The hedge fund's newly acquired bonds would be valued at 80.5, showing a 0.5 point loss which was the result of the transaction costs of deploying new capital. Because hedge funds are commingled vehicles, meaning that all the investors' capital is managed in one large pool, the cost of investing this new capital is borne by all the investors in the fund proportionate to the amount they have invested. Transaction costs are socialized, and are rarely shared equitably across all investors. It's very hard for any hedge fund investor to measure this, not least because NAVs are usually produced monthly and it's not a trivial task to measure that kind of detail. And market-impact costs are themselves imprecise estimates; in this case, the hedge fund's buying may force the price up to 81 bid, 82 offered, muddying the assessment of whether there was a true cost to the hedge fund.

However, over large numbers of transactions the market-impact costs will average out—indeed, they really have to, since the dealer's profit in quoting a two-way market in those bonds is the bid/ask spread. It's their fee for providing liquidity, for holding inventory and being a counterparty to the trade. The trading profits of large Wall Street banks are often the market-impact costs for hedge funds, particularly in bonds and foreign exchange where no formal exchange exists. This is in part how JPMorgan's Rates business or Goldman's FICC (FX, Interest rates, Commodities) generate so much revenue. For example, in 2010 JPMorgan's Investment Bank generated $15 billion in revenue in Fixed Income (within which they include Foreign Exchange and Commodities), following $17.5 billion in 2009 when markets were bouncing back from the credit crisis (in 2008 revenues collapsed to only $2 billion). Since bonds and FX do not generally trade on an exchange, these revenues are largely from acting as market maker to clients and counterparties, including hedge funds. Goldman's equivalent business (FICC) generated $23 billion in 2009, approximately half of the company's total revenues and a record. Markets recovered strongly but liquidity hadn't yet fully returned, which created the perfect environment for market making. Following the public outcry over Wall Street profits, Goldman stopped breaking out their results this way in 2010.

## How Some Investors Pay for Others

I had an opportunity to see firsthand how trading impacts the performance of a hedge fund and how those costs are inequitably shared. In 2003 we invested in a market-neutral hedge fund run by Peter Algert and Kevin Coldiron, Algert Coldiron Investors (ACI). Peter and Kevin had both worked at Barclays Global Investors (BGI), one of the best-known users of quantitative models to invest in large, highly diversified portfolios of equities. Peter and Kevin had decided to leave and set up their own firm, and we agreed to provide the initial seed capital to start their fund. Peter has a PhD from UC Berkley and headed research, while Kevin was in charge of portfolio management. Our provision of seed capital to their new fund gave us a share in the fees they would earn on all subsequent investors, common practice in such situations.

If they could grow the fund, the return on our investment could be augmented substantially through this fee-sharing. Kevin and Peter are both terrific guys. Kevin had spent some time living in London while with BGI and had an MBA from the London Business School, so he had some familiarity with England's national sport and my team Arsenal. Over the years Peter and I had gone skiing together with other members of ACI. We were invested with ACI for seven years until the terms of our fee-sharing arrangement expired. It wasn't all a walk in the park, and 2007 to 2008 was obviously particularly difficult. But the two of them were unfailingly professional and hard-working, that rare combination of talented investor and driven business builder. Our investment with them was in total a good experience.

In May 2003 the fund was launched, with $25 million of capital from JPMorgan. One of the benefits of being a seed investor is that you can often negotiate advantageous terms, and amongst the many things that we required was complete transparency of the portfolio on a daily basis. This meant that we could see all the trades they did and the daily profit and loss (P&L) so that we could monitor our investment almost as closely as ACI could themselves. I was somewhat startled on reviewing the first day's trading results to see that we were down 0.48 percent. While not a substantial loss, for a one-day change in value it was still pretty significant. Market-neutral investing as explained to us by Kevin and Peter involves a great deal of quantitative analysis to arrive at a portfolio of longs and shorts that's highly diversified and is designed to extract a very small edge or *alpha* across a large number of positions. Losing almost half a percent in one day seemed at odds with this.

It quickly became clear as we discussed the first day's results with Kevin that the commissions and market impact costs of investing in several hundred small-cap stocks was largely responsible. As a "quant" shop, ACI was well armed with some fairly sophisticated analytical tools, and they were quickly able to break down a single day's result into its various components. Our conclusion was that it was a one-time event, an unavoidable consequence of investing our capital. The portfolio would of course require regular rebalancing as prices moved and their models gave new signals, but nothing that would compare with the initial start-up.

At the end of the month, ACI received its first "non-seed" investment, of another $25 million bringing the fund's size to $50 million. This was a solid start and the early feedback from many other investors who were watching ACI and considering their own investment in the fund was largely positive. We all felt very good about near-term prospects for growth. On the first day of the second month, unsurprisingly, the fund was down around 0.24 percent. The new $25 million had been invested, and had incurred transaction costs similar to those we had examined on our own first day. But because we were in a commingled vehicle, we were bearing our share of the costs of the new money coming in.

In fact, it doesn't take much thought to realize that in any fund the early investors pay for a disproportionate share of the market-impact costs. The bigger your share of a fund, the more your own investment will pay the freight. An early investor can wind up losing quite significant value through this sharing of transaction costs. And of course, needless to say, the process repeats itself on the way out. If a fund is shrinking and you happen to be one of the last to leave, you'll be paying a greater share of the expense of those leaving, as securities need to be liquidated in order to generate cash to meet redemptions.

This is one of the little-known secrets of the hedge fund business. Hedge fund managers understand this issue all too well. Their investors rarely do. While many investors will have a conceptual understanding of transaction costs, they rarely spend much time focusing on it, not least because it's hard to obtain accurate information. However, few hedge fund investors have stopped to think about how the timing of their investment in a hedge fund as well as their percentage of the overall fund will affect their own results as others investors come and go. The open-ended structure of hedge funds, with its commingled assets, is what makes this possible. It's very convenient for everybody as long as the investors don't look too closely. And hedge fund managers have little reason to go into what can be an arcane topic. But this is why mutual funds, with their open-ended structure, place constraints on frequent withdrawals or in some cases charge investors fees when they invest to cover the expense of investing their capital.

This problem only became clear to me as a result of seeing the daily results of ACI. This is why so few investors are familiar with it, because they don't have the opportunity to watch a hedge fund's daily activities in such a close-up fashion. Growth in ACI was going to be a drag on our performance through these shared transaction costs. Over time the effect would become less significant as their assets grew and the costs were spread over a larger pool of investors. And of course in our particular case because we had negotiated a share of the fees they earned from all their other clients, overall we stood to benefit dramatically from their success. The fee-sharing benefit was worth substantially more than the shared transaction costs. But our situation was unique—all the other investors, including the $25 million that followed a month after launch, would suffer these costs inequitably; not based on what it had cost to invest their capital, but instead based on when they invested and the decisions of others. The costs are shared unevenly.

ACI's structure was utterly normal. There was nothing wrong in how the fund was set up or managed, and thousands of hedge funds operated the same way and still do today. For my part, believing that the hedge fund industry might benefit from an improvement, we persuaded ACI that they should charge investors a fee for entering and a fee for leaving. The fee (typically 0.5 percent) would be based on the likely cost of investing new money or raising cash to meet a redemption, and would naturally be paid to the fund and not to the manager. In this way, the entry/exit fee would offset the transaction cost and result in a more equitable sharing of costs. Such an arrangement was very unusual but other hedge funds have adopted the practice. *AR* magazine ("Paul Singer's Elliott Management, which has had a bang-up year, is instituting a performance fee for the first time," 2009) noted in 2009 that Paul Singer's $16 billion Elliott fund had been charging a 1.75 percent entry and exit fee to investors, presumably to defray the costs of deploying new capital (for new investors) or raising cash (for redeeming investors).

Kevin and Peter were somewhat uncomfortable only because they felt it would be a difficult issue to explain to new investors, but they agreed to go along because they understood the unfairness of the current system and felt, as I did, that it was worth trying to fix. But they did find the vast majority of investors failed to initially grasp the concept. Most investors thought it was simply a fee that would hurt their returns, and didn't fully appreciate the idea was simply improved fairness. These transaction costs were happening to the fund anyway regardless of whether or not there was an entry/exit fee. I had hoped that we might begin a trend toward more fair and open treatment of hedge fund investors, but I have to concede that few hedge funds saw the need to change and few investors demanded it. If hedge funds were operated as closed end vehicles like private equity and did a single round of fund raising, everybody would be treated fairly. Alternatively, separately managed accounts ensure that each investor absorbs only the costs related to their own investment because they're not in a commingled pool with others. Both would be an improvement.

## My Mid–Market or Yours?

How market-impact costs are allocated should be an important issue for every hedge fund investor. But the NAV itself, the value at which investors enter and leave the fund, can be manipulated in ways that are rarely clear to either current or prospective investors. The first thing is that "mid market" or "fair value" are by their nature only good-faith approximations of value. In every market the price at which participants can buy is different from where they can sell; how different they are is a basic measure of how liquid a particular market is. A hedge fund could have two NAVs, one for redeeming investors (the "Bid NAV") based on where the manager can liquidate securities to provide the necessary cash, and one for new investors (the "Ask NAV") reflecting the costs of deploying new money. The difference between the two would be approximately equal to the liquidity of the hedge fund's underlying investments. It would be a bit cumbersome, but would make explicit what is currently only implicit in reported results. For hedge funds investing in large-cap public equities, developed market government bonds, or foreign exchange, bid/ask spreads are small and the Bid NAV and Ask NAV would be quite close to one another—maybe 0.25 percent or so. Hedge funds in corporate bonds and small-cap stocks might use a spread of 0.5 to 1.0 percent. And the amount of leverage employed would also play a role.

It's helpful to illustrate with an example. Consider two hedge funds that invest in convertible bonds. One has no leverage and the other employs leverage of 5 to 1, which is to say for every $1 it has in capital from clients it borrows an additional $4 and buys $5 in bonds. To make it simple, we'll assume that each fund only holds one bond, and the price of that bond with dealers in the marketplace is 99-101 (i.e., can be sold to a dealer at 99 or bought from a dealer at 101). Conventionally, the hedge fund would mark to market its portfolio (of a single bond in this case) at mid market or 100. However, in many cases as long as the bond is valued in between 99 and 101 that would be defensible as a "fair value" for the security. That would be sufficiently precise, "good enough for government work" and if all that's being done is to provide a valuation it's very reasonable. However, transactions take place based on a hedge fund's NAV every month, and an investor has as much stake in a correct NAV as he does in buying any other investment at a fair price.

Table 6.1 shows how the reported NAV of the hedge fund could vary depending on where within the 99-101 bid/ask spread for the bond it is being valued.

**Table 6.1**  Unleveraged Hedge Fund

|  | Low NAV | Fair NAV | High NAV |
| --- | --- | --- | --- |
| Bond Price Used in Valuation | 99 | 100 | 101 |
| Value of Assets | 99 | 100 | 101 |
| Value of Debt | 0 | 0 | 0 |
| **NAV (Assets—Debt)** | **99** | **100** | **101** |

In this simple case, of course the stated NAV of the hedge fund directly reflects the price used to value the bonds. The NAV can vary by 2 percent, which is the same as the range between bid and ask for the bonds held by the hedge fund.

Now let's look at the same math in the case of a hedge fund leveraged at 5:1, not uncommon in the convertible bond market, shown in Table 6.2.

The leverage magnifies the sensitivity of the NAV to the price being used to value the bonds. Quite small differences in bond valuation, when viewed through the prism of leverage, can create as much as a 10 percent difference in NAV. As long as the bonds are being valued within the bid/ask spread, which is to say within a normal range, there's really nothing wrong. However, for an investor putting capital into the levered fund or redeeming from it, the difference is certainly not trivial. While the example is obviously simplified so as to illustrate, the point is nevertheless that investors have a very real stake in how the NAV is calculated. Less-liquid securities are more prone to this type of manipulation.

It's unlikely to be consequential for developed market equities (other than perhaps small cap), sovereign debt, or foreign exchange. Corporate bonds of all credit types including mortgage backed securities are where the potential for abuse exists, and the use of leverage (as

**Table 6.2**  Leveraged Hedge Fund

|  | Low NAV | Fair NAV | High NAV |
| --- | --- | --- | --- |
| Bond Price Used in Valuation | 99 | 100 | 101 |
| Value of Assets (5 × Bond Price) | 495 | 500 | 505 |
| Value of Debt | 400 | 400 | 400 |
| **NAV (Assets—Debt)** | **95** | **100** | **105** |

shown above) can exacerbate the range of plausible NAVs quite dramatically. Probably the best that an investor can ask is that it be done
consistently and most logically at the middle of the bid/ask spread.
However, it's a rare hedge fund Private Placement Memorandum
(PPM) that will define with such precision how this should be done,
and in some cases it is ripe for abuse.

## The Benefits of Keen Eyesight

In 2004 we met Howard Needle and David Harris, managers of Acuity
Partners, a convertible arbitrage hedge fund. Howard and David had
worked together before at Bank of America, and Acuity had been in
business about six months by the time we met. Howard was the more
personable of the two, and for good reason was more focused on marketing and describing their strategy to clients and prospects. David's
manner was somewhat brusque, intending perhaps to be a little intimi-
dating. In short, he was a typical trader—opinionated, strong-willed,
but also smart and quite likable as you got to know him better. After
spending some time with Howard and David over a period of weeks
we felt their prospects were good. They just needed some additional
capital to supplement what they had started with, which was largely
their own money. We negotiated a seed investment in exchange for a
share of the fees on future asset flows.

　　After a solid start, their performance began to lag. They had produced some strong results in their early months when they were small,
but the convertible bond market's rally had lost its energy and as the
months passed Acuity was steadily doing worse than its peers. Seed
investors sometimes agree to lock up their capital for an initial period
of time, so as to guarantee stable capital for the hedge fund manager.
At the same time, to protect the investor in the event that performance
is just terrible and he wants to exit early, there are typically minimum
performance targets that the investor and hedge fund agree upon from
the outset. We had agreed to lock up our capital with Acuity but had
negotiated the ability to exit early if their performance was particularly
weak. During the first few months of 2005 they continued to struggle,
and much as we wanted them to succeed we were starting to worry

about the trigger on our early exit provision. By May, the convertible bond market was seeing increasingly heavy selling, and even though Acuity was running a hedge fund they were not able to hedge against falling bond prices and their losses accelerated.

In early June we had a meeting of our investment committee and decided that we had little choice but to exercise our escape clause. The HFRI Convertible Arbitrage Index was already down 6.5 percent for the year, which doesn't sound like much compared with a bad period for stocks but was by far the worst period of performance in its history. Convertible arbitrage was about hedging away market risk and extracting modest but regular profits. The market was in complete disarray.

David tried to convince us that the timing was bad—and indeed the market had continued to deteriorate. However, in our original fund raising discussions with investors we had carefully described the provisions we intended to negotiate with new hedge fund managers, including the ability to extricate ourselves from a lock up on our investment. We felt that, while the timing was not great, we had an obligation to follow through on an element of our risk management, and we put in a redemption notice on 50 percent of our capital. The terms of our investment allowed for an intra-month redemption. Since an official NAV from the administrator was required on which to calculate the proceeds owed to us, the administrator duly calculated the fund's value based on the bond prices provided by Acuity.

Our investment had lost several percent in value in just a few days from the end of May when the last NAV was calculated, until the date of our redemption. This is where the seed investor's ability to access actual positions and trades is so critical to truly understanding what transpired. We complained bitterly to Howard and David about the sharp drop in value. They pointed out how weak and illiquid the market had become, conditions that were at their most dire at precisely the time we were exiting. We felt that the bond prices used had been unfair, and in response David sent us a spreadsheet listing detailed quotes that he had received from various dealers. As we analyzed the data, we began to understand what had taken place. We had daily valuations on Acuity's portfolio and compared them with the daily values of the convertible bond market.

The results were eye-opening. Through late May and into early June, Acuity's daily values had tracked the broader market indices reasonably well. Then, at the time we communicated our intention to redeem until the point five days later when the precise NAV was calculated, Acuity's valuation had deteriorated much faster than the index. On the precise day that half our capital was redeemed, the gap between Acuity and the benchmark was at its widest. In the days following the difference narrowed as Acuity's fund value retraced its steps. David Harris had even provided us with a spreadsheet from the day the relevant valuation was done, and more often than not the bonds Acuity owned were being valued on the bid side of the quoted dealer market, rather than at mid market. The valuation of their portfolio had been biased down at the moment it would reduce the value of our redeeming investment, and then allowed to return to its normal level.

We told David what we believed had happened, and that we felt we'd been treated unfairly. He was outraged, and strongly argued that they'd done nothing wrong. The market had been exceptionally weak, and he was pricing conservatively. What made it worse was that although he'd used bond prices close to or on the bid side of available quotes, in many cases they had chosen not to sell bonds at those prices. They were able to do this because they didn't need to raise cash to return our capital. The fund already had sufficient cash to pay us out. So our redemption value had been calculated on the basis of sharply depressed prices even though Acuity never had to sell bonds at those prices. In effect, using the example of the leveraged hedge fund earlier in the chapter, they had valued the portfolio using a bond price of 99 but never sold any bonds at that price. Our loss from receiving less than we should have from our redemption was the gain of the rest of the investors in Acuity, including of course Howard and David.

We never agreed on the issue. We felt very badly treated; Howard and David were adamant that the entire process had been fair. We had been exposed to the hedge fund manager's ability to value the portfolio, and even though the valuation was always defensible legally as being within the bid/ask spread of the underlying bonds, we felt we'd been had. Fortunately, we were able to turn the trick back on them two months later. Convertible bonds rebounded sharply, and Acuity began a dialogue with several investors about quickly investing while compelling values were available. We still wanted to withdraw the other half of our capital, and we guessed that to the extent they could bias their NAV higher or lower by late August, they'd want it to be higher to emphasize the strong recovery in their performance following the market's early summer slump and rebound. To return to the leveraged hedge fund example, with the possibility of new inflows and with investors paying close attention to their monthly performance, we thought they'd more likely value bonds at 101 rather than 99. We were right, and our final redemption in late August was at buoyant prices since we'd identified where we could align our interests with the manager.

Acuity did nothing wrong in legal terms. The bonds in their portfolio were, as far as we could see, valued within the bid/ask spread. The fund's documentation on valuation required no more, as is usually the case. Some hedge funds will assert that they value their holdings on the bid side because this is more conservative. It does produce a lower NAV, and therefore a lower and more conservative valuation for existing investors. However, this should be false comfort because it also means that new investors come into the fund at a "conservative" (which means low) NAV. Since the new capital received will have to be deployed, the manager will either have to buy more of the securities already owned, incurring transaction costs shared by all the investors, or use the cash for new opportunities which has the effect of diluting the existing investors' share of current holdings at the bid side of the market. In effect, existing investors sell a pro-rata share of their holdings to the new investors at the bid side of the market, hardly fair if there exists a 1 to 2 percent bid/ask spread. My central point to Acuity had been that whether they typically valued securities at the bid side of the market or at mid-market, they ought to be consistent. Switching methods depending on whether investor flows were into the fund or out of the fund was not right.

Subsequently I had some fascinating conversations with other hedge fund industry investors about whether what they did was right or not. People are very confused about this issue—my conclusion was that it's not well understood by most investors. There's a view that, if bonds have to be sold to meet a redemption then the portfolio should be valued using prices where those sales took place. The logical corollary is that if there are inflows the bonds in the portfolio should be valued at prices where additional securities could be bought so as to maintain consistent exposures with the new money. Others felt that it really depended on whether or not Acuity had decided to sell to meet our redemption or had instead elected to use cash already on hand, thus increasing the risk of the portfolio to the remaining investors at a highly advantageous time. There was no consensus and this is because the issue is not well understood as well as being unique to hedge funds.

The combination of an open-ended fund structure, allowing inflows and outflows without having to create a new legal entity, combined with less than highly liquid underlying investments, creates all kinds of opportunity for the manager to just shade the valuation in the direction most beneficial to him. The use of closed end funds, separately managed accounts, or entry/exit fees are all solutions that would ensure fair treatment of all investors with respect to one another. However, few investors understand the intricacies of the issue; few managers care to explain it, and over time, somehow hedge fund returns turn out to be just a little bit disappointing. This is part of the reason.

## Show Me My Money

Another area where investors have been way too accommodating is position transparency. An article in the *Financial Times* ("Poll highlights fears on industry secrecy," 2009) found that two thirds of investors in a poll cited either graduated fees or increased transparency as necessary inducements for them to invest. You'd think that for 2 & 20 you'd be entitled to see where your money is. But hedge fund managers have been so effective at convincing investors they don't want to look under the hood that I've heard investors note approvingly the restricted transparency a manager provides. Some of the arguments make sense. There's always the risk that even if the detailed position information is only shared with existing investors under signed confidentiality agreements it'll somehow leak out. A manager with a short position in a stock that becomes widely known risks others buying long positions or covering their own shorts anticipating that the manager will have to cover at a loss. This would of course hurt all the investors in the fund, and so withholding information protects the investors. The same can be true where a manager is in the middle of establishing a large position in a security and wants to maintain a low profile until it's complete.

But in far more cases it's because the manager wants to obscure the actual sources of profitability. This can be to preserve some intellectual edge or proprietary trading model whose insights might be revealed along with the positions, or to make it harder for investors to precisely analyze what risks are being taken and therefore the quality of the returns. In fact the hedge fund industry provides less information to its clients than any other area of asset management. Institutional asset management of equities and fixed income has long operated through separately managed accounts which allow the client to see precisely where there money is as well as ensuring they only pay their own costs (unlike the earlier example of ACI).

Away from traditional asset management, alternative asset managers such as private equity and real estate routinely disclose the names of the companies or real estate projects in which they've invested. But hedge fund managers have been able to buck the trend. One enormous benefit to the industry has been the relatively little quantitative analysis that investors can do on their own to assess how they're making money and if they're making enough to justify the risks they're taking. The opaque nature of the hedge fund investment means that it's often impossible to see what actual risks are being taken. The best an investor can do is compare returns after the fact with how markets moved and then make assumptions about whether those same relationships will hold. As a result, hedge funds have been able to market themselves as delivering uncorrelated returns and investors have had little to go on beyond the returns themselves. Since portfolio theory and common sense will make an uncorrelated investment more desirable, the limited information provided by hedge funds has played to this directly and with great effect. In fact, one very large and successful hedge fund placed constraints on how much information an investor could share even within its own research department.

In one case, a particularly secretive hedge fund insisted that only a select group of individuals at a fund of funds investor was to review the reports the manager provided. This investor was even required to implement changes to its database software so as to comply with these demands. Non-compliance was to risk being fired as a client, illustrating the lopsided relationship that has long existed between the industry and its paymasters. But significant risks are being taken by hedge funds, as shown so spectacularly in 2008. While hedge funds clearly didn't cause the crisis, they performed substantially worse than they should have and in many cases imposed restrictions on investor withdrawals to support their own business survival as much as to protect their investors from dumping holdings at a large loss.

Traditional asset management measures returns compared with a benchmark. Information Ratio compares the excess return a manager earns over a target benchmark with the standard deviation of the excess return, and as long as the benchmark is relevant will differentiate between good and weak performance per unit of risk. In addition, precise knowledge of the positions held allows factor analysis to examine subtle risks (such as an overweight toward interest rate sensitive stocks or consumer demand). Meanwhile hedge fund analysis has remained a mostly qualitative business. Sharpe ratio is often used, but it was designed for use with stocks as part of the Capital Asset Pricing Model (CAPM) and most academic literature notes that it's not much use on hedge funds which don't behave like stocks because they're not stocks. Most of the number crunching that hedge fund allocators do uses historic returns because that's all they have. While transparency has clearly improved since 2008 through greater demands from investors, it still falls far short of what they receive elsewhere. The entire industry from consultants to pension funds has largely accepted the more limited information they currently receive, which perhaps helps explain the weak results they've earned in aggregate.

A good friend of mine, Andrew Weisman, once wrote a wonderfully provocative paper called "Informationless Investing and Hedge Fund Performance Bias." It's a fascinating thought experiment that illustrates why you need to know where your money is. In Andy's paper he describes a trading model whose returns are simulated through a Monte Carlo simulation. In other words, he calculates the results his trading model would generate over thousands of possible outcomes where the mathematical relationships amongst stocks, bonds, and so on are similar to history. This is a commonly used technique to value complex securities. The paper then plots the returns on the trading model as if it was a hedge fund, and the resulting chart looks like every investor's dream. A very stable but attractively high return with apparently little relationship with stocks, bonds, or anything else an investor might have in his portfolio. It naturally has a high Sharpe ratio and if it existed every investor would want an allocation.

Incidentally, Bernie Madoff's fund looked very like Andy's model, which should have been a clue to more people than Harry Markopolos (whose book, *No One Would Listen: A True Financial Thriller* detailed his conclusion that Madoff was a fraud based partly on his returns). But the Informationless Investing model is simply selling options. It sells out-of-the-money put and call options on a regular basis, incurring limited risk to short-term moves in the market but exposing itself to ultimate bankruptcy. The simulation illustrates that the strategy will probably "blow up", or lose a third of its capital, within seven years (that is, the probability of it not blowing up drops below 50 percent at the seventh year). And of course few would choose to be simply short options, although the returns do look very attractive for a time. In fact, as Andy notes, the average expected life of the model (or the time until it will probably destroy itself) is longer than the life of the average hedge fund. While easily dismissed as a theoretical exercise, there have been cases in which a fund shorted options during the month only to cover the positions just before month end when investors were provided "position transparency."

Informationless Investing describes two other theoretical trading techniques that can produce attractive returns but either understate the level of risk being taken or ultimately lose substantial capital (or both). Although the paper was originally published in 2002, its insights are timeless and every hedge fund investor would be well served to ponder its implications.

Receiving comprehensive details on the positions held by one's hedge funds would seem to be both a reasonable request and also a sound way to see exactly what is going on under the hood. While disclosure has improved in response to investor pressure, current practice still falls short of complete openness. It's sometimes argued that if provided with every last detail through a daily computer download, many investors would be simply overwhelmed and unable to process the complex data received so as to obtain useful information from which they'd have a better understanding of their investments. There's certainly some truth to this as well. Our own experience with seeding managers can illustrate this; as we began receiving daily position downloads from our new, small managers we encountered all kinds of problems getting the data in the right format. Things like this can be incredibly mundane but time consuming at the same time. The software that we used to crunch data on each fund's positions needed to receive the data in a certain format, while the manager might be using a different system (perhaps provided by his prime broker).

Figuring out where the errors were and correcting them could easily distract from more important tasks for both the manager and us, and in fixing it we certainly learnt more about data mapping than we ever wanted to. Then there's the question of what you do with all the data once it's been processed. Looking at the overall risks for a portfolio of hedge funds that straddle multiple strategies may require combining risks from, say, a global macro fund trading currencies with a convertible arbitrage fund. It's not really clear that combining them gains you any more insight than looking at each separately given how unrelated their strategies are, and we soon concluded that transparency was best used on a manager-by-manager basis so as to deepen our understanding of what was going on. Not having complete access to exactly what you own creates additional risks.

## Summary

Understanding what any individual hedge fund has done can be surprisingly complicated once you decide to dig into the details. The industry has long provided far less information to its clients than any other asset class, and while transparency has improved, investors remain surprisingly quiescent. As seed investors receiving daily reports on trades completed, we were able to improve our understanding of the investments we were in and see whether we were receiving fair treatment or not. It can be hard, painstaking work making sense of several months' worth of transactions and the resulting questions may not all be comfortable ones. In some cases being presented with a comprehensive record of activity may well feel like you're holding a firehose not a glass, and many complex trading strategies would likely be incomprehensible if viewed without the manager as a guide. In some respects less than complete transparency suits both; investors needn't struggle with intricate and subtle trading strategies, while managers preserve some secrecy and perhaps mystery around their returns. In addition, if the fund suddenly suffers large losses, the investor wasn't at least in theory armed with enough information to have anticipated it, reducing the legal risk it may face for having remained in the fund. The ultimate result is that of a very unequal partnership, in which the manager retains the upper hand. Investors are partners in a purely legal sense, but the relationship can sometimes feel like something very different.

# Chapter 7

# The Hidden Costs of Being Partners

Investors in hedge funds are usually referred to as partners. In fact, as a strict legal definition they very often are, by virtue of being limited partners (LP) in the normal LP structure that houses the assets and liabilities of a hedge fund. But hedge fund managers will often refer to their clients as "partners" as if to suggest true business partners sharing upside and downside together. Being partners can almost seem like being friends, and business friendships are part of the investing fabric. It's a clever double entendre, because the investors are really clients but referring to them as partners suggests a unique venture in which "we're all in this together." And of course it's true that if the manager isn't making money the clients aren't likely to be either. But beyond the drag of the typical 2 & 20 of a large hedge fund, there are some more subtle costs that are borne by partners in a hedge fund.

## Limited Partners, Limited Rights

The legal structure requires an Offering Memorandum (OM) or Private Placement Memorandum (PPM) which describes the investment strategy, terms, background of the principals, and all the risk factors. Although required reading for every investor, the investment strategy is not normally well described in these documents; the marketing presentation is typically clearer. However, the OM will normally incorporate broad flexibility for the manager to shift strategies and asset classes. Since they're written by lawyers retained by the hedge fund manager (though the costs are ultimately passed through to the investors), reading through one of these documents makes it clear that the manager invests in almost anything. Funds also have a Limited Partnership Agreement (LPA) or, if structured as a corporation, an Articles of Association. These documents describe the rights of the investors ("limited partners" in an LPA, shareholders if a corporation) and the many rights and few obligations of the manager.

Investors have far weaker rights than shareholders in a public company. For instance, it's often extremely difficult to fire the manager, or even to request an annual meeting of the shareholders. In fact it may be impossible to even establish the identities of the other shareholders. In 2009 *Alpha* magazine ("Fine print in hedge fund charters makes it hard to oust poorly performing directors," 2009) reported on just how governance rules could be stacked against the investors. "Some investors are finding out that even if they have support from their fellow shareholders, they do not have the collective power to remove the current board and appoint new, independent directors," says Roger Hanson, a principal at Cayman Islands-based DMS Management, a director-placement firm. Rules under which shareholders in a fund could call a meeting varied widely, with some funds requiring as few as 10 percent of the shareholders to request one while others needed as many as 75 percent. There were few common standards.

Cognis Capital was a European credit fund based in London that we seeded with $20 million in December 2003. The terms of our investment included a share of all the fees (both management and incentive fees) paid by all of the other clients, which was a typical arrangement for a seed investor such as ourselves. This meant that as Cognis grew we stood to make potentially more money from participating in their business success than from our investment in their credit fund. The managing partner Myra Tabor was formerly of Royal Bank of Scotland, and she set up the fund with two colleagues. Myra is not your typical hedge fund manager. Probably less than 1 percent of hedge funds are run by women, and Myra additionally stood out because of her strong Welsh accent and jaunty personality. In fact, one salesman I spoke to who knew her well commented admiringly of Myra that she, "Didn't buy all the crap I was trying to sell her when I was at Merrill Lynch." Although their office was in Mayfair alongside some of the wealthiest hedge funds in the world, Myra remained very down to earth and unaffected by the success she subsequently enjoyed. She's a huge fan of English football and over the years we went to some games together. She showed remarkable drive and resilience which never flagged, even through some difficult times in 2008, and was invariably upbeat and positive. She and her partners were all known to JPMorgan and had a good reputation. The fund performed well and grew steadily, riding the bull market in credit with great success until 2007. Then both her partners suddenly left within a couple of months of one another for apparently unrelated reasons.

One of them, Paul Hollowday, was a former officer in the British Army, and in a most surreal conversation in late 2007 told me he had lost the motivation to work and needed some time out to "find himself." He wasn't burnt out as much as bored. I struggled to reconcile the military man, whose former commanding officer had regarded his leadership so highly with the quitter who was jumping off the ship at the first sign of trouble. It didn't make any sense, and he must have realized that some bad investments (including a catastrophic one he'd personally negotiated in a German industrial company that was ultimately written off completely) were going to drag the fund down. In any event, he left and after a few months of soul-searching was incredibly re-hired at another hedge fund, Zais. The other partner, John Sullivan, also abandoned ship several weeks later, informing Myra in an e-mail the day she arrived in the United States on a long planned marketing trip. I told her she had to turn around and go home, that it wouldn't make any sense to meet with investors when her investment team was falling apart around her, and she reluctantly flew back to London the next day.

Meanwhile, over the next several months, valuations continued to deteriorate. Many of the investments Cognis held turned out to be substantially less liquid than previously thought, and in the Summer of 2008, faced with withdrawal requests in excess of cash on hand, they were forced to suspend redemptions. The hedge fund had become in effect a private debt fund, and it became clear investors would receive their capital back only when the manager was able to find buyers for securities that at the time nobody wanted. By then Cognis had been a very good investment for us. Our seed arrangement had provided a share in the fees other investors paid, and strong returns combined with steady growth in assets under management (AUM) had driven up the value of our stake. In fact, we had been regularly withdrawing some of our capital since continued profits caused our Cognis investment to grow too large. By the time performance turned down in 2007 and 2008 we had already withdrawn more than our initial $20 million investment.

## Friends with no Benefits

Over the next two years following the suspension of redemptions investors waited while Myra tried to liquidate some of the portfolio. Schedules of anticipated distributions were issued and revised, and it became increasingly clear that turning the investments back into cash was going far too slowly. It was hard not to feel sympathy for Myra; she'd lost her two partners just as things were going downhill even though they'd all shared responsibility for the investments they'd made. No doubt Myra had made some poor decisions and in the final analysis she was head of the business with overall responsibility for results. We spoke regularly as she tried to sell individual securities and meet growing investor calls for some liquidity. Although financial markets rebounded shortly after Lehman failed in September 2008, the substantial rally in high-yield credit during 2009 and 2010 failed to have much impact on Cognis. The Credit Suisse European High Yield Index returned 76 percent during this time, a rally that passed Cognis by.

Clearly they held some investments that were beyond the help of a recovering global economy. Finally in September 2010 Myra announced that she had found a buyer for the portfolio; Paul Capital, a private equity firm, specialized in buying broken hedge funds from their investors in exchange for cash, albeit at a healthy discount to the current stated value. In this case they had offered 67 cents for every $1 invested, which came as quite a shock to many investors who had been led to believe the monthly NAV they received was a fair assessment of value. It highlighted the false comfort many draw from a monthly NAV when it collides with the brutal reality of the market where transactions can actually be done. Although Myra had developed strong feelings of loyalty among her clients, the drawn-out disposal and ultimate loss of value unsurprisingly left many feeling poorly treated. It also illustrated how limited are the rights of investors. While Paul Capital had been given an opportunity to review the portfolio in detail before making its offer, none of the current investors were afforded the same opportunity.

Since Myra was to stay on as the manager she was conflicted and therefore unable to express an opinion on whether the proposed trans-action was a good one for the investors. In fact, because a lower price paid by Paul Capital would increase their potential profit it had the perverse effect of also increasing Myra's potential to earn an incentive fee from them. However, the investors were never permitted to know the complete details of Myra's own agreement with them, and Paul's interests were to see that Myra was sufficiently compensated to see their investment paid off. The unpalatable choices presented to investors were to accept 67 cents in cash for every $1 invested without having any idea what the portfolio was worth or even what was in it, or to remain invested but agree to provide additional capital which was required to restructure some of the current holdings.

On top of this, although a small number of investors did organize themselves into a group to press for more information, they were unable even to force an extraordinary general meeting (EGM) of all the inves-tors to discuss the proposal, and Myra was under no obligation to call such a meeting herself. The fund had a board of directors, but few were convinced that they'd acted as the fiduciary representative of the inves-tors that their role required. Rupert Dorey, the lead director and a resident of the Channel Islands who made his living sitting on the boards of investment companies, appeared to be little more than Myra's employee. As far as we could tell all his information came from Myra, and he gave every impression of wanting to wrap up the transaction quickly, ending his involvement as the independent representative of by now very unhappy investors. Board memberships of hedge funds can be easy money until you have to do some work.

In fact there was little evidence that the Board had done any independent assessment of the transaction at all. The hedge fund Cognis ran had transitioned from high-yield bonds with annual liquidity into a portfolio of distressed assets with no known timeframe for its liquidation and the subsequent bounce in financial markets had completely passed them by. Myra argued that she was doing her best to raise cash as requested by many investors, and that there were no other good options. As frustrating as the experience was, the basic problem was that too many bad investments had been made prior to 2008. The credit crisis had revealed the weakness of their credit analysis. Some thought that Myra should keep managing the portfolio for as long as it took to sell everything, although she'd spent two years with limited success trying to do just that. Many hedge fund managers, faced with the prospect of not earning an incentive fee following a period of poor performance have just closed up shop only to relaunch soon thereafter with a new fund, reset high water mark, and new investors. Although Myra couldn't plausibly start a new fund without first resolving the old one, she had at least stuck with it and tried to recover some losses rather than immediately sell at distressed prices and move on with her life.

However, the sale to Paul Capital revealed the limited practical say investors often have over how their interests are handled even when the hedge fund manager is no longer unequivocally on their side. The governance rights in the documents didn't include the right to see the portfolio or knowledge of who the other investors were, and the rushed timeframe precluded an EGM. The investors deserved the same information that Paul Capital had in order to decide for themselves whether taking a one-third reduction in value was fair, particularly because Myra couldn't provide impartial advice given her ongoing role. Directors of hedge funds may hold as many as 20 or more directorships. In this case they were selected by Cognis and took no visibly active role. Removing Cognis as the manager, similar to stockholders firing the CEO, was implausible without the ability to organize a meeting of all the investors; although this option should have been made available, it wasn't. There were certainly other hedge fund managers qualified to take over responsibility and give investors the opportunity of doing better than an immediate one-third loss of their remaining capital. However, the Board saw no reason to do it. Meanwhile Myra, unable to dispose of her portfolio, changed her clients instead and now stands to profit if it rebounds in value from the discounted price at which Paul Capital acquired it.

From the point in July 2008 when redemptions were suspended, investors realized a loss of 47 percent on their capital, in spite of the fact that credit markets bottomed out within a few months and roared back over the following two years. As a seed investor our experience was quite different. Our investment had grown through sharing in the fees of all the other investors, and as a result we'd made regular withdrawals to limit the size of our exposure. By the time 2008 rolled around we'd already redeemed more than our initial investment, so although the subsequent 47 percent loss hurt everybody, disciplined risk management meant we were still nicely profitable overall.

However, nobody else had shared in the fees the way we had, and unsurprisingly other clients of Cognis I spoke with were deeply unhappy at the outcome. Many investors are surprised at how little say they have over their own money. Nothing illegal took place, and of course any investor who was unhappy with the deal could have voted against it or perhaps sued under Cayman law (the legal domicile of the fund). Recognizing that there were simply no good options available and weary of the extended delay in retrieving their money, investors swallowed hard, approved the transaction, and reasoned that they had better opportunities to pursue. Meanwhile the manager retained control in spite of widespread dissatisfaction with the outcome, illustrating the substantial weaknesses facing clients in the widely used commingled partnership structure when things don't go as expected.

John Sullivan, who had abruptly fled Cognis in 2007 when he no doubt anticipated the impending disaster he had helped perpetrate, later re-emerged in 2011 running the Wiltshire Credit Opportunities Fund.

In his marketing materials he claimed to have made 22 per cent annually while at Cognis, figures sharply at odds with the actual results and regarded as ludicrous by at least one former colleague.

Even in May 2011, some two and a half years after the collapse of Lehman Brothers and the psychological low point of the credit crisis, a substantial portion of investor assets remained out of reach. Hundreds of hedge funds had suspended redemptions as permitted in their fund documents so as to avoid dumping securities into markets that in many cases had ceased to function. While this can be a reasonable way to protect all the investors in a fund, you might think that once the crisis has passed normal terms would be reinstated. *InvestmentNews*, a weekly publication targeted at the investment industry, reported that $100 billion of investors' capital was still being withheld under the exceptional moves made in 2008. At around 5 percent of the industry that's a surprisingly large chunk. It reported some large and previously very successful funds were among those hanging on to their money, including GLG Partners, Harbinger Capital Management, Highland Capital Management, and RAB Capital.

The extended delay in receiving back their requested cash has caused frustration and no doubt difficulties for a number of investors. As a result, a shadow market has developed in which investors can sell their hedge fund investments to other opportunistic players at a steep discount to face value. Tullett Prebon, a large money broker, and Hedgebay are two firms that specialize in this market. *InvestmentNews* noted that in a recent month Tullett Prebon's average trade took place at a 58 percent discount. In other words, investors were willing to take as little as 42 cents on the dollar in order to get out of the hedge fund. This is an unreported downside faced by many investors but not picked up in industry returns. Although it's probably a stretch to say that $100 billion in reported assets is really only worth $42 billion simply based on this report, the popular indices don't include the more than 50 percent realized loss incurred by those investors choosing to sell out into the secondary market. Assuming all the losses relate back to 2008 when most such withdrawal restrictions were imposed, that would reduce returns for an already bad year by a further 3 percent, to −26 percent.

## Watching the Legal Costs

From a purely structural standpoint, hedge funds are odd creatures. They're a hybrid, combining several features to form a structure that's part mutual fund, part private equity. In one respect they're like mutual funds in that many are open-ended vehicles with regular valuations. The open-ended nature makes it easy for investors to enter and leave the fund, since the fund's legal structure remains intact and they simply issue more shares (or create new limited partner interests if a partnership) to accommodate inflows. Similarly, when capital is withdrawn, the manager eliminates the shares or LP interests represented by the departing capital. Most hedge funds are created in such a way that their structure can accommodate inflows and outflows indefinitely.

It's attractive to investors, since it allows them to add to their investments over time in the knowledge that they can redeem at a time of their own choosing (within the liquidity constraints of the fund itself). This is also convenient for the manager since creating the legal entity that will be a hedge fund is time consuming and costly. In fact the legal work supporting hedge funds is a lucrative source of profit for Wall Street law firms. Sometimes it seemed to me as if they charged as if each document has been written from scratch, although in reality there's no doubt plenty of copying and pasting from previous work (as I once suggested to a lawyer during a billing dispute she was having with one of our seeded hedge funds). In truth though, the legal documents would be far more expensive if all the work was original. Drafting legal documents can often seem expensive, until they're needed to resolve a dispute at which point a thoughtfully drafted clause can render the legal fees easily worthwhile. But it can also be hard to manage the costs involved as they're occurring. I always felt it was perfectly reasonable to ask a lawyer what a project will cost, but this happens too infrequently and few lawyers encourage it.

One manager we knew received a $250,000 bill from a top New York law firm for work that had originally been estimated at between $50,000 to 100,000. Of course the clock starts ticking immediately when you call your lawyer, and the focus is naturally on accurate advice rather than minimizing costs. But the differential top firms charge for what is becoming a generic legal structure is another example of the costs facing investors, since these costs are passed along in the form of operating expenses of the fund. In fact they're typically amortized over five years and deducted from the monthly returns investors receive. In most cases they're inconsequential when spread over AUM of several hundred million dollars or more, and in any event are far less than the management fee. But if a fund fails to grow and ultimately winds down before the five years has elapsed over which the legal costs are expensed, the last investors remaining in the fund can be left with a hefty bill. As seed investors we were well aware of this and wanted to avoid a situation where our $20 million investment along with, say, $2 million from the manager were all that was left to absorb the remaining costs on a fund that was being wound down. So we insisted managers agree that any remaining expenses would not be charged to us, since ultimately the decision to close a fund or press on lies with the manager. On at least one occasion this provision saved our investors some money.

As hedge funds have moved beyond their early focus on public equities to just about every tradable asset class, they have retained their open-ended nature. But as they invested in less-liquid markets and took more concentrated positions, the easy entry/exit of the open-ended fund structure became modified with gates, lockups, and other mechanisms. The enormous growth in the industry and the search for new inefficiencies and markets led it away from the relative transparency and immediate liquidity of public equities. They branched into less liquid markets and strategies that more appropriately belonged in closed end, private equity vehicles since the easy liquidity of developed public equity and debt markets was not being provided to investors in these newer strategies. However, the open-ended fund structure had served both managers and investors well, and was largely retained, albeit with constraints on investor withdrawals as an acknowledgment that the underlying instruments weren't as liquid.

Distressed debt is a sector that doesn't really belong in an open-ended fund structure. The underlying instruments can be illiquid and not always freely traded. The bid/ask spread is certainly wider than for traditional assets. In recent years the open-ended structure has been twisted and bent to accommodate investment strategies that are far removed from the original long/short equity funds. Hedge funds have been formed to invest in private loans (known as direct lending), unregistered securities for which a liquid, continuous market most certainly does not exist, and life insurance policies—a somewhat distasteful strategy in which policyholders sell their policies to a third party at less than their ultimate value. The policy pays out to the investor when the original policyholder dies, and therefore the price the investor will pay is based on actuarial analysis of when the policyholder is likely to die. Since getting paid ahead of schedule is positive for the investor, premature death is a source of higher investment returns. Such transactions are quite legal, and their proponents point out that the result can be an immediate cash payment for the individual which might well be more useful than waiting for the more normal conclusion of the life insurance.

However, I've never liked the optics of making money from someone else's severe misfortune (i.e., death). In agreeing to a cash settlement, the policyholder is in effect betting against the actuarial tables; surviving beyond his statistical life expectancy will render his sale a sound investment decision just as it will decrease the investor's return. Celebrating long life just seems a wholly more agreeable way to live ones's own, and poor investment returns to investors in life policy funds probably make the world a slightly better place. The point here though is that life policy funds are not hedge funds in any conventional sense. They clearly can't hedge, and the notion that a monthly NAV is anything other than a best guess at the value is not credible. But hedge fund investors are where the money is to be found, and the open-ended structure allows investors to come and go, creating apparently more liquidity than exists for the life policies themselves. Hedge fund investors are often so keen to examine new and potentially profitable strategies that they've increasingly accepted greater illiquidity risk. Since a hedge fund is not a legally defined term, if you can somehow squeeze your investment strategy into a box that makes it at least appear like a hedge fund, the idea can be pitched to the gatekeepers of that capital.

It's amazing sometimes how an entrepreneur looking to raise money will try and tailor his strategy to fit where the money is. In 2000 I was involved in Internet strategy at Chase (just prior to the merger with JPMorgan). We met a group called ePrimus, run by Joe Baumann and Tom Jasper. Joe had been a prominent figure through the early growth of the derivatives business, for a time heading ISDA, the industry trade group. Tom was well known as a senior fixed income specialist at Salomon Brothers and was a co-founder of ISDA. Chase had a small pool of capital set aside to make strategic investments in Internet start-ups that we thought could have a far-reaching, transformational impact on our business. The investments were in the $2 to $10 million range, nothing like the size that our future merger partner JPMorgan was committing through its own Internet division LabMorgan. ePrimus came to see us looking for capital on the basis of its groundbreaking use of the Internet to help them manage a portfolio of credit risk (much of the activity involved credit derivatives rather than bonds, but that's another story). It quickly became clear that their success was dependent on credit decisions, and the use of the Internet was of secondary importance to their overall success. However, they knew we were looking at Internet investments and so they positioned their venture accordingly. Not long afterwards of course the funding for most Internet startups dried up as the dot-com bubble burst, and ePrimus quickly dropped the "e" and the focus on Internet and subsequently raised money from more conventional sources.

## Summary

Partnerships can be great when a business goes well, and when they don't everybody learns why the small print matters. 2008 was a true wake-up call for many investors who found that the impact of a financial crisis on their rights was to reveal how ephemeral they could be. Lessons were learned, and based on the rebound in AUM mutually satisfactory solutions to these issues and others were reached. But while having your capital unwillingly locked up for an extended period can be aggravating, at least you know where it is. For if there's one thing worse than an inability to redeem your investment, it's an inability to locate it.

# Chapter 8

# Hedge Fund Fraud

Hedge fund investors already face many traditional investment risks (market risk on each manager's holdings, liquidity risk, credit risk through each fund's choice of counterparty, operational risk in terms of accurate valuation and efficient trade execution). Then there are other risks more specific to hedge funds, such as style drift if a manager deviates from his original specialization and perhaps outside his recognized expertise in search of higher returns, and business risk in that the hedge fund manager needs to run a profitable business or the investor's time spent on due diligence will be wasted as his capital is returned. But sitting on top of all these concerns as the investor analyzes a hedge fund investment is the possibility that the entire enterprise is a sham and that he will one day suffer a complete loss of capital. It should be a source of no small embarrassment to the hedge fund industry that there is enough material to justify its own book of frauds.

## More Crooks Than You Think

*The Hedge Fund Fraud Casebook*, written by Bruce Johnson, examines industry frauds from 1968 to 2000. The very existence of such a book serves as a warning to all hedge fund investors. You can carefully analyze a manager's investment process, consider the subtle ways that his inclusion in a portfolio of hedge funds will affect its return, Sharpe ratio, value at risk, and other risk statistics. You can run historic analysis to calibrate whether a 3 or 4 percent weighting is more appropriate. And hanging over the entire exercise is the inestimable possibility that in fact it's a Potemkin hedge fund, and that the result may be a total loss with the consequent shredding of investor relationships, business model, reputation, and career prospects. Amazon.com fails to provide any matches for "private equity fraud" or "mutual fund fraud," although of course plenty of public companies (Enron, Worldcom, and Tyco Industries to name a few from recent years) have ripped off investors.

But hedge fund investing exposes the investor to an additional risk that's almost nuclear in its ability to visit devastation on its victims, and competent due diligence includes many steps to confirm the veracity of a manager's presentation. CastleHall Alternatives is a consulting firm whose business is dedicated to helping investors avoid "operational risk," a wonderfully anodyne way to describe fraud. CastleHall is meeting a real need—they don't have to warn their clients about possible hedge fund fraud, the industry regularly generates sufficient examples to concern any investor. CastleHall maintains a database called "HedgeEvent," and it consists of 327 "events" from inception through June 2009 with an estimated financial impact of $80 billion! Even without Madoff (which they estimate at $65 billion although ultimate losses were much lower), CastleHall identifies losses from operational failure of $15 billion (Hall, 2009). And it excludes episodes such as Long Term Capital Management and Amaranth, which lost substantial sums through a combination of incompetence and hubris. CastleHall goes on to estimate that approximately 3 percent of the universe of hedge fund managers has experienced an "operational event." It suggests this is pretty good and concludes that "operational failure is material, but not pervasive."

But investors are typically meeting new managers on a regular basis, often every week. If dining at a local restaurant carried a 3 percent chance of food poisoning you'd probably eat elsewhere. Simple probability theory suggests that if a hedge fund investor meets and considers 52 managers in a year, the probability is 79 percent that at least one of them is crooked.[1] It's not a stretch to suggest that every year most investors unwittingly meet with at least one fraudulent manager.

Bruce Johnson's book lists 100 cases of hedge fund frauds, although it is by no means an exhaustive list. Of the 100 cases selected, 69 percent resulted in losses to investors totaling $2.5 billion (in 2005 dollars), arguably not substantial although the size of the hedge fund industry was only $237 billion at the end of 2000 where the study ends. In fact, the book doesn't seek to provide a complete account, and since 2000 there have been many more contemporary episodes including Samuel Israel, Ed Strafaci (discussed later in this chapter), and of course the legendary Bernie Madoff.

The sheer scale of the Madoff deception is such that he surely deserves immortality by becoming an adjective. Ponzi schemes are so named after Charles Ponzi, who successfully (at least for a while) used later investors to pay off early ones thus maintaining the illusion of superior investment skill until the edifice collapsed in 1920. If "doing a Madoff" enters into common financial discourse it will have to represent a substantially more sophisticated conspiracy incorporating chairmanship of a major exchange (Madoff was of course chairman of Nasdaq during 1990 to 1991 and again in 1993) and regular rejection of new clients (creating an air of exclusivity). Investor account statements at the time showed $65 billion in largely fictitious balances, so

---

[1] A 3 percent probability that a manager is a fraud implies a 97 percent chance that he's not. $0.97^N$ (where an investor holds N meetings a year) is the probability of not meeting a fraud all year. So $1 - 0.97^N$ is the probability of meeting at least one. Assuming one meeting per week, the one-year probability of meeting a fraud is: $1 - 0.97^{52} = 1 - 0.2052, = 0.7948$ or 79 percent.

Madoff represented more than 3 percent of the entire hedge fund industry in 2008 (although by 2011 the trustee Irving Picard estimated total cash losses at $20 billion [Bernard Madoff Overview, 2011]). Madoff typically isn't included in the returns for that year reported by most databases—the year was already quite bad enough.

There is no book listing 100 frauds in mutual funds, private equity, or real estate, and while frauds and dishonest behavior have occurred in just about every commercial activity, the hedge fund industry has managed to subject its investors to a disproportionate number. As well as being catastrophic for the investor, allocating to a fraudulent manager can often be career ending for the allocator (no doubt rightly so). If you're looking for the right investment vehicle with which to commit fraud, hedge funds are an obvious choice. Their private limited partnership structure, often-obscure trading activities, and unregistered status all help the would-be con artist. Publicly traded stocks and bonds are registered with the Securities and Exchange Commission (SEC), and while registration certainly doesn't preclude fraud the required public disclosures make it less likely, particularly with the small army of short sellers out there constantly searching for crooked companies to expose. Mutual funds and closed end funds are also required to register and make public disclosures. Meanwhile, within the world of alternative assets (which includes private equity and real estate as well as hedge funds) your private equity manager typically tells his investors which companies he's bought and those that are interested can often meet with them or do other fact finding. Real estate funds invest in tangible assets such as buildings that can be visited and are hard to fake. It's not that any one of these is immune; it's just that they're all more difficult choices. If you want to run an investment scam it's hard to beat a hedge fund as the vehicle of choice. Avoiding frauds is unfortunately a necessary component of successful hedge fund investing.

Once you've been lied to and confronted an individual over it, you realize that just about anyyone can surprise you. Over the years I've come across several situations with managers where things turned out to be different than they appeared, and although through judgment (and sometimes luck) I've avoided losing money, each episode can serve to shake one's confidence in the integrity of the investment industry.

# Madoff

I had my own opportunity to invest with Bernie Madoff back in 2003 and 2004. Fairfield Greenwich is the now infamous fund of funds that channeled large amounts of capital to the Madoff Ponzi scheme. We found ourselves in a meeting with representatives of the firm discussing Madoff and his remarkably consistent returns. As we probed during our meeting for the definable edge that was responsible for this success, the Fairfield marketers described the set-up: Madoff operated two businesses, a brokerage firm that executed trades for clients and a money-management firm that ran the hedge fund. The brokerage division and the asset-management division shared common ownership and, it was explained, might sometimes be executing the same trades. The rules on *front-running* exist to protect clients from brokers who place their own orders in the market ahead of the client. What they were describing sounded odd, but such meetings are not intended to review whether a manager is fully complying with all the relevant regulations. It's assumed that he is, and the nature of such meetings is that to question something on the basis of its potential illegality is generally not appropriate. The conversation moved on to other topics and concluded uneventfully.

Years later, when Madoff was exposed and the tragic losses suffered by so many investors were becoming clear, I thought back to that meeting. Although the Fairfield marketers never used the term front-running and didn't suggest anything illegal was taking place, it occurred to me that this was probably what they themselves believed was supporting the consistently successful results of Madoff's hedge fund. Madoff's investors, including those brought in by Fairfield Greenwich, were profiting at the expense of the brokerage clients. The further attraction of such a scheme to a hedge fund investor could be that they'd be the passive beneficiary of such activity, with no liability for doing anything illegal yet still able to profit from it.

That was our only meeting with Fairfield Greenwich or anybody related to Madoff. At the time we just didn't pursue it, largely because we knew we'd be unable to negotiate the preferential economics that we sought. But the apparently free movement of information between the brokerage and asset management divisions, with its consequent potential to disadvantage some clients at the expense of others, would have made it unlikely to receive serious consideration. Regardless of the potentially convenient "passive" nature of the investment for the investors, it's not something we would have felt comfortable pursuing.

It's probably no coincidence that the long list of victims of Madoff didn't include any of the large Wall Street firms. Goldman Sachs, Morgan Stanley, Citigroup, Merrill Lynch were all notably absent, no doubt because even the most cursory due diligence revealed some insurmountable issues. Some have asked whether Wall Street firms knew about Madoff and should have done more to expose him. For my part, in one meeting I learned just enough to conclude that this wasn't an investment that would make it through the first stage of JPMorgan's predictably thorough due diligence review, but not enough to be at all comfortable crying fraud or contacting the SEC.

Of course, as it turned out Madoff was not front running his brokerage clients at all, but simply fabricating results and taking out their cash. And while we'll probably never know, I suspect that Fairfield Greenwich believed what they were telling us. They were of course victims themselves, and somehow in their own all-too-brief review of Madoff's activities had concluded that front-running clients were the source of his edge. If so, this was the basis on which they had been happy to invest $7 billion (Bray, 2010) of client capital. While the many individuals who trusted Bernie Madoff were unwitting, and often tragic, victims, there is a sweet irony in that professional investors, having willingly invested so as to profit unfairly from other clients, instead became victims themselves.

## Know Your Audience

This was the most famous example of fraud with which I've had a passing encounter. There are other far less notorious cases, and while they range from brazen to almost clever, together they illustrate how thorough investors need to be before entrusting their capital to an unregistered vehicle run by an unregistered firm in a poorly understood strategy. Integral Investment Management came to us on one occasion with a foreign exchange (FX) arbitrage strategy. This was of particular interest because all of our investment committee members worked in the FX division of Chemical Bank, and as a result we felt we had more than just a passing familiarity with the markets that Integral traded. At that time I oversaw the trading of interest rate derivatives and forward FX across all the major currencies in New York. Interest rate parity is a condition in financial markets that links the future value of a currency to its value today through the interest rates in the two currencies. Just as the price of oil (and most traded commodities) to be delivered in six months is based on today's oil price plus the cost of six months' storage and the relevant six-month interest rate, forward settlement FX rates are determined by today's spot rate and interest rates.

The FX markets are highly efficient at maintaining equilibrium amongst these moving parts, since if any component moves out of line a riskless arbitrage profit is available. Part of our FX business at Chemical Bank (and in any large FX trading business) was to exploit such opportunities, and taking advantage of the brief moments when things move out of line typically requires a well-constructed trading operation.

So we sat there in disbelief as Conrad Seghers from Integral Investment Management carefully explained how the FX markets were broadly inefficient, and that as a result he was able to use interest rate parity to generate risk-free arbitrage profits. He even showed us a successful back-test of his strategy (naturally all simulated back-tests shown to investors are highly profitable because they don't involve actual money) to support his claims. Initial meetings with hedge fund managers are usually deferential affairs, with polite interest and the presumption of good intentions on all sides as the due diligence process unfolds. I am afraid on this occasion my observance of protocol failed me and I sat aghast as Conrad calmly described the profits he was able to unlock from the biggest, most efficient market in the world. I asked him if he realized that all the major banks focused substantial human and financial capital on exploiting such opportunities all day long in every financial center. After hearing his response I bluntly told him I felt his assertions were simply not credible and that I didn't believe him. The meeting ended uncomfortably, and while we never pursued an investment with Integral it came as no great surprise when in 2006 Seghers and his partner James Dickey were both convicted of fraud in a Federal court in Texas, having raised over $70 million from various investors (SEC Litigation Release 19631, 2006).

## Accounting Arbitrage 101

Some hedge fund investors have all too frequently carried out only the most cursory due diligence before investing. Chris Goggins was a proprietary FX trader at Chase in the 1980s and 1990s. Chris was from London but had lived in the United States for much of his career, and we met following the merger between Chase Manhattan and Chemical Bank. Chris was a likeable individual, typically good humored and always ready to discuss his views on the market quite openly. He often possessed an unusual insight or perspective and had a wide number of market contacts with whom he would share opinions on FX markets. Chris was also a highly profitable trader on a consistent basis. His daily trading results were uncannily steady, as he combined short-term trading with core interest rate and currency bets that he would hold for many months. Chris's steady profitability over a number of years during the 1980s had earned him the respect of senior management, and as a result his unconventional hours were quietly tolerated. Chris would often arrive at work at 10 a.m. (unusually late for an FX trader), and would often stay until 6 or 7 p.m. Chris was seemingly a reliably profitable trader.

The problem was that Chris Goggins's steady returns were the result of his ability to manipulate the bank's accounting system. Chris traded in two related areas of the FX market—cross currency swaps and long-dated forward FX. There were often opportunities to arbitrage between the two, and Chris's mandate included making profits from such trades. However, this required that he use two separate accounting systems since neither one was capable of booking both sides of these transactions. In order to avoid having to manually combine reports from two different systems so as to analyze his overall risk exposures, the bank had agreed to let Chris enter a hypothetical transaction between the two accounting systems whose sole purpose was to transfer risk from one to the other and therefore allow a consolidated view of exposures in one place. These hypothetical risk-transfer trades of course only existed within Chase's accounting systems and as such it was critical that they only be used to transfer risk and not change the overall trading results.

Unfortunately, the monitoring of these trades was weak, and as a result Chris was able to generate hypothetical gains and losses which he used to offset the normal daily swings in his trading results. This was how he delivered such consistently reliable trading profits. He could use his manipulation of the accounting system to smooth out the normal daily swings in profit and loss. Steady returns are almost always preferable. Over time though, as has happened too often in recent history, the cumulative result was that his actual results were overstated, ultimately by $60 million (*New York Times*, 1999). Joe Jett's 1994 fraud at Kidder Peabody relied on an accounting system flawed in its reporting of zero coupon bonds, and Nick Leeson similarly exploited Baring's accounting system when his losses on Nikkei stock index futures brought down the entire bank in 1995.

Chris knew that bank accounting systems had been exposed before. He was not the perennially successful FX trader the bank had long believed him to be. How must Chris have felt as Jett and Leeson were each exposed earlier in the 1990s? In hindsight, his occasional hangover-induced late start to the working day is a little more understandable. In 1999 the accounting flaw was finally identified; Chris was confronted and his career at Chase was over. The bank even had to file a brief explanation with the SEC and the story was reported in the *New York Times* on November 2, 1999, under the headline "Chase Manhattan must cut its revenue after discovering some non-existent trading profits."

Chris never faced criminal prosecution, though no doubt he had to forfeit whatever prior bonuses had not already vested. Although he had in effect committed fraud by misrepresenting his trading profits, such cases are often hard to prove before a jury. The bank's accounting systems were clearly embarrassingly weak, and he was able to leave without a criminal record. To the extent that Chris had been paid bonuses in past years based on his inflated trading results, he had of course defrauded Chase Manhattan and its shareholders.

Amazingly, some years later, Chris set up his own hedge fund called Victory Investment Management, in Summit, New Jersey, where he lived. It represented staggering chutzpah on Chris's part that he could bring himself to market his money-management abilities after being publicly identified as misrepresenting his trading results. It was also evidence of the almost complete absence of any meaningful due diligence by whichever investors entrusted their money to him. The circumstances of his departure were public information, and within Chase's FX division the story was widely known. It was reported in the *New York Times* (in fact, even today a search on their web site for "Goggins" in 1999 will still reveal the story). It wouldn't have been hard for even cursory research into his background to reveal his past.

## Checking the Background Check

We always carried out background checks on managers before we seeded them. Although we followed a careful and thorough due diligence process using many of our own sources both within JPMorgan and outside the firm to vet people, we maintained a healthy insecurity that there might be some important information we didn't have. Paranoia in investing can be a useful form of self preservation as long as it's not so strong as to become debilitating and prevent any investments being made at all. In practice most investment decisions are inevitably made with less-than-perfect information.

We regularly used a private investigator (we'll call him Magnum, not his real name) to review all public sources and some proprietary channels on each manager. Magnum consistently reported back on each successive manager with a clean bill of health, combining public sources with almost unimaginable access to the human resources (HR) departments of major banks where each manager had worked. It was extraordinary to hear personnel records describing an individual as "highly talented, a regrettable loss when he resigned" and so on since HR records are supposedly completely confidential. Through several investments in new hedge funds Magnum consistently found nothing that should prevent us from moving ahead with each investment. It seemed that our own screening process was so thorough we were weeding out any dubious characters well before they reached the level of serious consideration. Each call with Magnum concluded in the same way, that our target was "clean."

After a while though, we thought it might be useful to run a check on Magnum himself. After all, while we were happy that each manager checked out, we had no way of knowing if he was really obtaining these confidential HR records from a surprisingly large number of banks and other sources. Magnum seemed to have extraordinary access, but was it too good to be true? What we needed was to run a check on someone that we knew had a bad past. Like Chris Goggins.

So we went ahead and ran our "test" of Magnum. He of course passed with flying colors, commenting that "we have some problems with this one" at the outset of the phone call during which he reported his findings. Naturally he'd quickly found the *New York Times* article, but in addition Magnum obtained a quite detailed description of Chris's accounting manipulation that was so accurate it could only have come from someone within Chase, perhaps from HR or the FX trading division. He further found that while both the SEC and NASD were aware of Chris's actions and had notes to that effect somewhere in their files, the CFTC (which in theory regulated Victory Investment Management) did not. And Magnum also discovered that the IRS, in their classification of taxpayers, had placed Chris in a higher risk category not normally used for salaried employees because he'd had to restate prior years' income.

We couldn't know why, but since Chris would have had to forfeit unvested bonuses from prior years as a result of being fired he might have had to reclaim Social Security taxes, which were typically withheld and therefore no longer owed if the bonus wasn't going to be paid. It seems no information is reliably confidential, and we were now 100 percent sure that the background checks we were receiving on other managers were reliable. Magnum was the real deal. It was a relief to know he was that good and quite sobering to see his access to information.

Perhaps 10 years later, with the changed regulatory environment that followed Madoff and the mortgage market collapse, Victory Investment Management would never be possible as a sequel to Chris's prior failure. And while Victory never grew to any consequential size, it was evidently successful in bringing on some investors, presumably on the back of the many years Chris enjoyed as an FX trader at Chase Manhattan. Perhaps fortunately for Chris and his investors, Victory was never a big success. In fact, in 2010 I played English football against him in a league (older men in their 40s and 50s who ought to know better) and Chris told me he'd finally had to close the hedge fund down because it was becoming hard to raise money.

## Politically Connected *and* Crooked?

Sometimes the connections a manager has can add legitimacy. In 2002 we were looking for interesting hedge fund seeding opportunities with which to launch our Incubator Fund. Ed Strafaci came with apparently strong credentials. Ed was managing a convertible arbitrage hedge fund at Lipper Holdings, part of Ken Lipper's business. Ken Lipper was well-connected within the New York political and social scene. He had been Deputy Mayor of New York City from 1983 to 1985, co-wrote the screenplay for the movie *Wall Street* (which starred Michael Douglas), and ran a hedge fund. Ed Strafaci was introduced to us through Chris Brady, who ran a boutique investment business called The Chart Group and was the son of Nick Brady (Treasury Secretary under President George H. W. Bush). Ed's initial references at least appeared promising. Ed described his growing frustration with Ken Lipper over business strategy and compensation, and said he believed the returns they had generated in convertible arbitrage trading could be replicated outside of Lipper. All they needed was seed capital to get them started. We decided to spend some time drilling down into Strafaci's strategy, and invited him to meet with one of our colleagues (Remi Bouteille) who was familiar with many of the convertible arbitrage hedge funds currently operating.

Remi is French, one of the many graduates of the elite universities in France that produce a regular supply of mathematically gifted graduates. In fact, the equity derivatives business is disproportionately filled with math alumni from L'Ecole Polytechnique just outside Paris. Remi is a smart guy whose manner can sometimes appear abrasive or condescending. However, I'd always found that his opinions were typically well supported by facts and analysis. During the interview with Remi, Ed repeatedly avoided being drawn into discussing the specifics of different hedging techniques. Remi was looking for numerical answers to demonstrate Ed's technical knowledge of his strategy, and Ed's answers were frustratingly imprecise and vague. Ed appeared mildly insulted by Remi's manner of questioning, no doubt feeling that his track record and connections ought to be sufficient to demonstrate his proficiency. Remi felt Ed was being evasive.

Following the meeting, Remi confidently and memorably declared that Ed Strafaci was most likely a fraud. I must confess I was not at all convinced that Remi was right. I thought Remi's cold and impersonal style was not conducive to drawing people out of themselves, and that he was reacting in part out of his frustration with Ed's imprecise answers. Ed also came highly recommended by Chris Brady who was eager to fund an independent Ed Strafaci but was also keen to have JPMorgan in at the outset as a partner.

Over the next few weeks we continued our research, carrying out discrete reference checks and drafting an investment proposal. And then the news broke that Lipper's fund had been misvalued by (as it later turned out) $350 million, and that Ed Strafaci the portfolio manager was to blame. Remi (who to his credit did not brag about this) was right in his assessment on the basis of a single interview. Ed Strafaci was subsequently convicted of securities fraud and sentenced to six years in prison. Many investors had invested with Lipper either without a thorough meeting with the portfolio manager, an indefensible omission or (perhaps worse) after meeting with Ed. Clearly few other investors had gone to the trouble of exploring the mechanics of the strategy in intimate detail, and had instead relied on Ken Lipper's oversight and Ed's folksy style.

## Paying Your Bills with Their Money

In 2004 we met Scott Stagg and Gary Katcher who were running 3V Capital. Gary had left Merrill Lynch to found Libertas Partners, a broker-dealer, and brought on Scott from Lehman Brothers because of his experience in distressed debt. Scott and Gary were smart and had come up with a novel way to raise capital for Libertas Partners. A broker-dealer often needs to hold inventory, since buyers and sellers don't always want to transact at the same time. In order to provide liquidity to its clients in distressed debt, Libertas needed capital so it could hold bonds when clients wished to sell them, even if only for a few hours or days while they found a buyer. Being a willing buyer when clients want to sell, and having bonds available when buyers want to buy, is market making and is an important element in the structure of most bond markets.

The problem facing Gary was that Libertas was small and raising capital from traditional venture capital investors to allow it to hold larger inventory was expensive. The cost of equity that most private equity investors wanted to charge was in their view too high. So Gary and Scott came up with a novel solution. Since hedge fund capital was seemingly abundant, why not start a hedge fund and have it hold the inventory for Libertas. They figured they could easily raise $250 million this way, and then they'd have enough capital to hold inventory and support Libertas. Clients of Libertas would sell bonds which would then be passed on to 3V, to be held until Libertas had a buyer who would then buy back 3V's bonds through Libertas. It was an ingenious way to access the capital available to hedge funds and use it in effect as venture capital. While we admired their out-of-the-box thinking and thought they had the industry knowledge to probably be successful, we had several problems with the structure.

Broker-dealers like Libertas, that transact on their own behalf, and investment advisors like 3V, that act on behalf of clients, have conflicting objectives and therefore need to operate at arm's length. The fact that they had overlapping control meant that the potential existed for 3V to buy bonds at a loss in order to support Libertas in its drive to build market share. The office layout was clearly designed to allow the two firms easy communication—indeed, that was the point of their business model. In addition, we recognized that our hedge fund investment would create value for Libertas, and we wanted to make sure that our investors would be fairly compensated for jumpstarting the broker-dealer.

We had several discussions around these topics, but ultimately the concerns we had over potential conflicts of interest as well as inability to agree on the economics stopped us going forward. Eventually though, other investors including Weston Capital funded 3V (which changed its name to Stagg Capital) and AUM reached $550 million by 2007 (Vardi, 2009). We never understood how other investors resolved the issues we had identified. Sadly though, the very conflict of interest that had concerned us came true when in 2009 their chief operating officer Mark Focht was convicted of grand larceny for transferring money between the hedge fund and the broker dealer which was ultimately used to meet payroll expenses (Vardi, 2009).

## Why It's Hard to Invest in Russia

When we first set up the Incubator Fund in 2001 we had few competitors. Although we rejected 99 percent of the opportunities that came our way, we were able to indentify some promising candidates. By 2006 competition amongst seed capital providers was increasing and we had started to consider opportunities outside the United States. Russia had never been high on our list—an emerging market dealing with the legacy of Communism where property rights and the rule of law seemed to follow a wholly different set of rules than in the west. In addition, there were so many stories of people being ripped off, whether by a cabdriver from the airport, a local gang, or the government itself. So we weren't planning to invest in Russia. But then we met two people that made us feel, well, if we were ever going to invest in Russia it would be with them.

The fund was run by two Americans: Michael McGuire spoke fluent Russian and had spent many years there in various commodity businesses; his partner Arthur Heath had a Harvard Law degree and had previously been JPMorgan's local legal counsel in Moscow. Their fund was named Triple Trunk, after a local tree in Michael's neighborhood. Of course their proposed investment strategy and business model would need to be thoroughly reviewed for viability, but at least in terms of integrity we were unlikely to find a better qualified pair. We spent many hours with them taking apart their trading strategy (which involved the trading of physical commodities), reviewing the risks, the business plan, funding needs, market outlook, and so on. We started negotiating a formal investment agreement with them that would govern the terms under which we would invest along with our participation in the financial success of the business. One of my colleagues, Andreas Deutschmann, traveled to Moscow to meet some of the banks they proposed to use as counterparties and to learn more about the specific opportunities.

And then, in a routine background check on Michael, we discovered that Chase Manhattan had placed liens on two properties that he owned for failure to repay a business loan. You might think that if one department of our bank had a commercial dispute with an individual it would be known to any other relevant department. But it's a huge company with appropriate information barriers between divisions and there was no known internal database from which we could obtain information on legal disputes between any other division of the company and a certain individual. Nonetheless, we had information highly relevant to our transaction, and confronted Michael with it in our next meeting. It is almost always a sobering experience to hear someone you believed to be honest admitting that it is not the case. While the legal dispute itself related to a loan Chase had made to a failed business Michael ran and didn't allege any dishonesty, his failure to make us aware of it clearly was dishonest. His memorable response was that you don't tell a new girlfriend all the bad things about yourself on the first date. We had wasted time, but happily not any investor capital. His partner Arthur Heath was devastated and claimed quite credibly that he had no idea of this element of Michael's past. Arthur insisted on buying us lunch at the Harvard Club by way of drawing a line under the episode, and we all moved on.

We even had a meeting with Paul Eustace, formerly of Tewksbury Capital. Tewksbury had pulled off a rare feat in the hedge fund industry—smooth transition management. Most successful hedge funds are so closely identified with their founder, who has invariably retained close control over the invested capital, that maintaining success when the founder retires is difficult. Monroe Trout had run a highly profitable fund in Bermuda for many years, and when he decided to retire the business moved seamlessly to his longtime deputy Matthew Tewksbury. The name changed, but at least for the investors little else appeared to. Paul Eustace came to see us and claimed he was responsible for the development and implementation of forecasting as well as trading systems while at Tewksbury which had contributed to their overall profitability. He told us he had been the Chief Operating Officer, had felt underpaid at Tewksbury, and was therefore leaving to set up his own firm.

Somehow, although Tewksbury was highly regarded, Paul's story wasn't convincing. We just doubted that he could generate the returns he claimed, even though he offered to provide former colleagues at Tewksbury as references. We didn't pursue it and he soon set up his new firm, Philadelphia Alternative Asset Management Co (PAAM). In 2010 he was indicted on fraud charges (United States of America v. Paul M. Eustace, May 6, 2010). Had we decided PAAM was an attractive opportunity, we would have contacted Tewksbury and presumably been advised to avoid Paul. However, we rejected him simply based on his trading description—we had little reason to think he was a fraud until much later. It never ceases to amaze me though how some people will quite readily lie and misrepresent their past, even when the risk of exposure is quite high. People can always surprise you.

## After Hours Due Diligence

Some of the shrewdest hedge fund investors I know have developed a sixth sense, an ability at self-preservation that uncannily steers them away from trouble. They may not be certain a manager is lying to them; indeed, they may concede that the individual is "probably good, just not a good fit for me." But today's successful hedge fund investors have avoided "headline risk" (what happens when an investor's hedge fund makes page A1 of the *Wall Street Journal* for the wrong reasons) and protected both their client's capital as well as their professional reputations.

In 2000 Michael Berger's firm Manhattan Capital Management collapsed after its efforts to hide $400 million in losses from investors were ultimately exposed. One friend of mine, a seasoned hedge fund investor, told me that he'd avoided Manhattan simply because of a conversation he'd had with a third-party marketer representing Berger's fund. Over drinks one evening the marketer had complained about one wealthy hedge fund client who was persistently late in paying the marketing fees owed. Eventually and after several drinks the marketer confided to my friend the identity of the delinquent client, and this information was enough for him to conclude that everything was not as it appeared at Manhattan. The hedge fund investor's due diligence toolkit includes some unconventional techniques.

Dishonest people unfortunately operate in all walks of life. Routine dishonesty in most businesses may mean inflated travel and expense (T&E) expenses, inefficient use of resources, and many other actions that can eat away at the return on an investor's capital. However, what sets hedge fund investing apart is how disastrous it can be if the investor has the grave misfortune to choose unwisely. A complete loss of capital is not out of the question, and it's these consequences as well as the unfortunate prevalence of dishonesty that adds measurably to both the risks and the costs faced by hedge fund investors. Hedge funds are the perfect vehicle if you want to defraud investors. The funds and the firms that run them are unregistered. Although the laws against fraud in the United States apply as much to hedge funds as any other activity, the SEC doesn't have the ability to carry out routine inspections of firms they don't regulate.

Hedge funds operate in the regulatory shadows, although in many other ways they are in plain sight. Other common features that make hedge funds convenient vehicles for dishonesty are the commingled nature of the capital (the investors' funds are all pooled) and the lack of complete transparency. While thorough due diligence can protect the investor from these features being used against him, it's still unfortunately the case that the combination of non-regulation, indirect ownership of underlying investments, and incomplete access to information are all attractive elements for the dishonest money manager. Best practices have changed somewhat in recent years in response to events, but whether the risks of fraud are measurably lower than in the past is something strenuously argued by the industry but ultimately not yet known.

## Summary

People can always surprise you. I believe that most people are fundamentally honest. But in business we typically deal with so many different individuals that if only a small percentage of the population is crooked you still need to keep it in mind. The statistics mean you have to "trust but verify" as President Reagan once famously said. Most of us place great stock in our ability to assess others and to judge character in another. Therefore there are few things more sobering than to find that someone you thought was honest is not, and to confront them about it.

An unfortunate feature of hedge funds is that if you want to defraud people, a slightly mysterious trading strategy with an apparently strong history of performance in a limited partnership structure generally outside the regulatory framework is one of the best ways to do it. It's not that hedge fund managers are inherently dishonest—far from it. Most of them are far too intelligent and in any case able to make substantial money legitimately. But the hedge fund industry has, sad to say, attracted more than its fair share of ethically challenged people. Committing fraud is simply easier there than in many other areas of finance. It's not a systemic problem, but it is an additional risk facing investors. Greater transparency and increased use of separately managed accounts can help protect the investor.

# Chapter 9

# Why Less Can Be More with Hedge Funds

**B**roadly speaking across the breadth and history of the hedge fund industry, investors have not fared that well. The amazing result is that if all the money ever invested had instead gone into Treasury bills, the investors would have been better off. Few outsiders initially believe it when first presented with this fact. Yet I've spoken with people who've dedicated most of their careers to the hedge fund industry and they are rarely surprised. This gulf in perceptions between the hedge fund industry and everyone else is a stunning indictment. Poor timing, weak analysis, and hefty fees have all contributed to this outcome.

Of course, saying that hedge fund investors in aggregate have done poorly isn't the same as saying everybody's lost money. This book shouldn't be interpreted as making that assertion, because it's plainly not true. Just as the average income tells you little about the range of incomes in a country, so it is with investing. However, most of us have assumed that the average in this case was pretty good, whereas it turns out to be pretty poor. But even though there are hedge fund investors who have done very well as clients, it's surprisingly difficult to identify them. I've looked for clients who have made substantial profits *as clients*, excluding any fees they've earned from others' money. This excludes George Soros, for example, whose fortune clearly began with fees earned from managing money. Over time as his wealth grew he became a substantial investor in his own hedge fund and no doubt his current wealth has been augmented by trading profits—but he clearly wouldn't have reached his current state without the "2 and 20" combination of management fee and incentive fee. Steve Cohen of SAC is famous for being such a talented trader that he was able to take fully 50 percent of the profits he earned for clients as his incentive fee and still generate consistently high returns. He, of course, eventually made so much money from this arrangement that an increasing portion of the money he was managing was his own, and clients became an unnecessary distraction. Eventually he gave back pretty much all the clients' money, preferring to focus just on managing his own.

Of course George Soros and Steve Cohen are examples of highly successful hedge fund investors. They've made substantial sums managing their own money as well as charging fees to manage others' money. Nevertheless, if they are the best examples of profitable hedge fund clients, then the industry looks increasingly as if it exists to serve itself. In that case, the purpose of hedge funds is to provide jobs and wealth creation for the industry professionals: managers, consultants, allocators, prime brokers, and other service providers. Can any commercial industry thrive, or even survive, if its clients aren't the fundamental reason for its existence, the purpose behind all this activity? In fact the long-lasting and spectacular growth of hedge funds in itself seems to refute the notion that they haven't added any value. In a capitalist system the market decides winners and losers, and since there are clearly so many providers of hedge funds that are winners, their continued presence can only be because they're providing something worth more than what they charge for it. It's possible we're measuring the wrong things in trying to establish value received by clients. Maybe investment profits in themselves aren't the sole yardstick.

## There Are Still Winners

There are plenty of investors that are happy with their hedge fund investments. Since the individuals that are clients have to be wealthy enough to be "accredited investors," they're not that easily tracked down. Very rich people maintain discretion about their financial affairs. But some institutional clients do disclose their results. University endowments such as Yale and Princeton (Sorkin, 2010), and public pension plans such as the California Public Employee Retirement System (CalPERS) have noted generally satisfactory results. And I have a number of friends solidly in the "high net worth" category who say their hedge fund investments have been very satisfactory. But for every $1 well invested there's another $1 that wasn't, since the results in total aren't good.

Hedge funds are said to provide diversification, and they certainly do. Most investors will happily accept a lower return on investments that are not highly correlated with their current portfolio, and of course there's a whole academic theory (the Capital Asset Pricing Model [CAPM]) which can calculate how much less of a return you need from those uncorrelated investments. It depends on how related they are to what else you've got, how likely the new investment is to go down when everything else is going down. The less likely it is that they'll move together, the more helpful it is to your overall portfolio, which means that they don't need to make as much to justify the investment; but in the CAPM world, whatever you invest in has to do at least as well as Treasury bills. If even over the long term the investment doesn't do as well as Treasury bills, then there's no point in having it.

On the other hand, if investment profits aren't the main reason to invest in hedge funds, it's hard to know what is. Certainly investors give every indication that profits are what they're after. It's hard to think of any other non-economic objective. Hedge funds don't really serve any other useful purpose. Of course, the Robin Hood Foundation that Paul Jones started years ago provides generous charitable support to a wide number of good causes, and while that's to the credit of the supporters of that charity and others like it, philanthropy is a happy by-product of hedge funds, not the reason they exist.

Perhaps because there has been so much wealth created by hedge funds, establishing how well clients have done receives less scrutiny than it might. The combination of a respectable long-run average annual return, (which ignores the fact that the best years were when the industry was small) with many extremely wealthy practitioners, is a powerful reason to join in.

Why have investors done so badly out of their infatuation with hedge funds? Whose fault is it that the results have been so skewed in favor of just about everybody—except the providers of the capital from which so much has been earned? What should investors do so as to restore some balance to the relationship? Can it be fixed, or will hedge fund clients continue to bet against a two-headed coin?

Some of the most talented investors in history run hedge funds (or have retired from doing so). The compensation assures that in a capitalistic system, those with the most sought-after skill maximize their own return on selling their services. Personally, I find a great deal to admire in the thought process of George Soros, as he concluded that Sterling would be unable to maintain its peg against the Deutsche Mark in September 1992 and then backed up his belief with enough money to break the Bank of England. His $10 billion bet netted a cool $1 billion, and in an interview around that time noted that on hearing the British government nearly borrowed a further $15 billion to support their currency, ". . . we were amused because that was about how much we wanted to sell" (Slater, 2009). While Soros earned few plaudits in the United Kingdom at the time for "breaking the Bank of England" as the tabloids coined it, this episode confirmed his legendary status as a hedge fund manager.

Who can fail to marvel at John Paulson, as this experienced merger arbitrage manager, with little experience in credit derivatives, identified and constructed dazzlingly high pay-off trades with remarkably little risk, to profit from the inevitable collapse in the housing market? The acute risk management judgment of Alan Howard, as he guides his portfolio of traders through successive crises with an incomparably deft touch, knowing just when to reduce risk and just when to press his advantage, is almost awe-inspiring. Bruce Kovner, David Tepper, Louis Bacon, and others at the top of the industry possess fantastic abilities and have been able to implement them across large pools of capital. Hedge funds are not short of investing talent—far from it. But star-struck investors have too often equated enormous financial success amongst managers with high returns for clients (though I should note that all the managers listed above are among the Top 10 most profitable *for investors*, according to research by Rick Sopher of Edmond de Roth-schild Group and reported in the *Financial Times* September 10, 2010). When I first moved to the United States in 1982 I noticed a subtle difference in attitudes toward wealth between Europeans and Ameri-cans. In Britain, an accountant/doctor/lawyer parking his S-Class Mer-cedes would cause onlookers to comment disapprovingly at how he must be ripping off his clients in order to afford such a car. In America, the same scene would cause most to conclude that the individual must be successful and therefore worth doing business with! Although hedge funds and their investors are global, the American attitude toward wealth, to staying close to winners, has prevailed, as with so many American values, as the world has become flatter (credit Thomas Fried-man, author of *The World Is Flat: A Brief History of the Twenty-first Century* for illustrating how values and technology are making the world smaller and flatter).

If there is such a thing as Hedge Fund IQ (HFIQ), or a quality which combines superior investment analytical ability, a trader's instinct for survival, well-developed commercial sense, and a highly competitive winning attitude, it would have its own brutal hierarchy. Hedge fund managers would be at the top, next would come the traders at banks who trade with them and against them (the best of whom move to hedge funds or start their own), after them would come those that invest directly in hedge funds (funds of hedge funds and other institutions), below them, the consultants that advise others on their investments, and, at the bottom, the trustees and investment committee members of the large institutions who have so recently added alternatives to their portfolios. All of these levels include highly intelligent people in the conventional sense and this description of the HFIQ hierarchy should not be regarded as demeaning to those not at the top. Golf includes players of wide-ranging abilities (thankfully for me!) and you don't have to be as good as the club pro to enjoy the game. Nor does mediocre golf ability say much about how well you play basketball. Hedge Fund IQ is a highly specialized, narrowly defined quality. Those possessing it in abundance run hedge funds, while the rest get as close as they can. You can play a round of golf with the club pro for money, but you'd better use your handicap to get fair odds. Hedge fund investors need to acknowledge they are unequal partners with their chosen managers and pursue negotiating strategies that compensate, or invest elsewhere.

If investors have done so poorly, whose fault is it? When looking at the split of profits between fees and returns and the extremely modest share of the pie retained by investors, it's tempting to condemn hedge fund managers as representing the worst excesses of Wall Street, exploiting markets, investors, and knowledge for their own benefit. The capital markets fundamentally exist to channel savings in directions where they can be most effectively deployed. Few would argue that the efficient allocation of capital requires the creation of today's hedge fund fortunes in order to be carried out effectively. But that philosophical question is for others. Investors are all voluntary clients. Hedge funds are meeting a clear demand from the market. And the vast majority of capital in hedge funds is provided by "qualified" investors, either individuals with sufficient net worth to be deemed "sophisticated" or institutions fully capable of accurate analysis. The fact that it hasn't turned out well is very largely the fault of the investors themselves. Faulty or weak analysis, performance chasing, shortage of skepticism, and a desire to be associated with winners without proper regard for terms have all caused the sorry result.

## Avoid the Crowds

The assertion that small, new hedge funds outperform larger ones is often debated within the industry. There is a growing amount of academic research on the topic and countless articles. The case for small managers is inspired by the fact that most of today's successful hedge funds began life much smaller than they are now. In addition, their returns were often higher. This is why there's such a gaping difference between overall profits earned by investors (since recent years' returns have been disappointing) and average industry returns (strong results in the 1990s were generated by a much smaller industry).

Being a small manager has many benefits. As with any entrepreneur launching a new business, the start-up hedge fund manager throws himself body and soul into the new venture working $24 \times 7$ to get it off the ground. This intensity of effort is critical, because if returns are not good in the short run, then, at least for this manager, there won't be a long run. Small amounts of capital are generally easier to trade, in that you can usually buy or sell as much of a security as you need without moving the market away.

Closed-end funds (CEFs) are a great example. These are like mutual funds, except that they have a fixed share count, so investors buy shares in the secondary market just like any other stock. Closed-end funds publish a net asset value (NAV) every day just like mutual funds, but since they don't issue and redeem shares every day to meet/accommodate demand, the price of their shares doesn't have to equal their NAV. In fact, the shares usually trade at a discount to NAV. Anybody who thinks the markets are efficient should check out the closed-end fund business. In the United States it's driven by thousands of retail investors who are looking for income. Many closed-end funds respond to this by making distributions in excess of their own investment income, which really means they're just giving you back your own money.

Trading closed-end funds is an interesting and obscure backwater of the financial markets. Liquidity is poor and, as a result, it's difficult to deploy much capital—but for small traders or hedge funds it can be a worthwhile area to research.

Suppose a closed-end fund has $100 and it's invested in stocks which pay a 2 percent dividend. The closed-end fund is earning 2 percent, and this is what the investors in that fund should really see as their yield (although the fund manager's expenses will take a chunk out of that, but we'll leave fees out for now to keep it simple). The manager knows that a 2 percent yield is not that interesting, so he makes the annual distribution $5, covering the difference with the capital in the fund. This $5 distribution results in a "distribution yield" of 5 percent and investors who confuse it for an actual yield think they are getting a good deal. I once had a conversation with a research analyst at a large Wall Street bank, and asked her why her research didn't describe the yield in cases like this as 2 percent rather than 5 percent. Acknowledging it was wrong, she nevertheless insisted that this was how the market (i.e., retail investors who know no better) thinks of yield and so she was simply following market practice.

Investors in closed-end funds are looking for steady income. Most stocks pay dividends that vary much less than their profits because the market rewards the predictable income this creates for investors with a higher stock price. CEFs are no different, and even though their actual returns are largely driven by changes in the prices of what they own, the payment of a regular distribution or dividend attracts investors who want stable income. But whereas a company whose dividend is not covered by its profits will, before long, reduce its dividend (and one warning of this is when a dividend yield is unusually high, indicating that the market believes it's unsustainable) CEFs work differently. Some funds, recognizing the appeal of a high yield, will make large distributions partly supported by the underlying investments. This will perversely make the fund price rise regardless of the long-term unsustainability of such a strategy, because buyers like the higher yield, even though a chunk of it comes from giving them back some of their own money. Eventually the CEF would have used up all its capital in supplementing its dividend and would be an empty shell, having returned all the money to investors. However before that happens they'll typically cut the distribution to preserve capital which invariably sours investors on the fund and sends its price lower. Whereas a high dividend yield on a stock can be a warning, in a CEF it's an invitation. It seems that no matter how many articles are written on the topic, investor behavior doesn't change.

Then there's the closed-end fund initial public offering (IPO). Everybody on Wall Street knows that you never buy a closed-end fund when it's being issued. This is because the underwriters take 7 percent of the proceeds as a fee, so if the fund is issued at $20 it immediately loses 7 percent of its NAV and falls to $18.60. It's a guaranteed loss, and yet, every closed-end fund IPO is evidence of the continued gullibility of certain parts of the investing public. Even the underwriters know it's stupid—I had another conversation with the capital markets group of a Wall Street bank, where they asked me if we had looked at any recent CEF IPOs. No, I said, they're all an easy way to lose 7 percent. This was quickly acknowledged and we moved on.

Boulder Total Return Fund (BTF) has played this game with great skill. BTF is run by a fellow called Stewart Horejsi in Colorado. His web site is intended to evoke Warren Buffett (of whom Stewart is a great admirer) and describes his long-term approach to investing, through seeking value and using low turnover. For a time BTF sported a high distribution yield—even though it was supported by returning investors' own capital to them. Earlier this decade BTF traded close to its NAV as it made regular distributions to investors. Then, in 2008, it did what no CEF should do—and eliminated its dividend. The price duly fell and a large discount opened up between NAV and price. Some managers regard a wide discount as a vote of no confidence in their abilities and take steps to close it (perhaps by buying back shares). However Stewart Horejsi recognized an opportunity and so has been regularly buying shares in the open market for himself and trusts that he manages. He correctly saw the persistent discount as an opportunity, and reinstating the distribution would simply make it more expensive for him to continue buying the shares. Sometimes an activist investor will get involved and will buy up enough shares to justify a board seat, where he'll threaten to force a change of management, unless steps are taken to increase shareholder value. But in the case of BTF, a substantial minority of the shares is owned by the manager and affiliated entities, so it's virtually impossible for an activist to gain a foothold.

Another sound rule of CEF investing is that you never buy funds at a premium to its NAV. Why pay $110 for a basket of stocks that are only worth $100? If you like them that much, just buy the underlying stocks in their portfolio. Nevertheless, people do it all the time, and in doing so, lock in poor or negative returns on their investments.

A closed-end fund is really nothing more than a company that invests in other public companies. They don't manufacture anything or provide any services; they just own stock in other companies. A CEF earns the investment returns on its holdings and passes on at least 90 percent of them to its investors. It pays fees to the money manager who oversees the portfolio. Valuing a CEF is not nearly as difficult as valuing an operating company like Microsoft or Kraft. It's worth whatever its stockholdings are worth, and CEFs regularly publish a NAV (similar to mutual funds).

Until I began researching closed-end funds I had never come across such an inefficient market. Retail investors do dumb things every day, whether it's participating in an IPO or buying a fund at a premium to its NAV (something you should never do). There are dozens of articles on the subject of CEFs with all kinds of sensible advice, and several books which discuss the persistent discount to NAV and why it exists. While there's nothing easy about trading (and in my experience it usually feels easiest just prior to a loss), if you pay close attention, you can find relatively attractive trading opportunities in CEFs, caused by many of the self directed but less sophisticated retail investors who predominate. The returns can be attractive, but the liquidity is limited. For instance, BTF only has a market capitalization of around $200 million and trades around $300,000 to $400,000 in value on a typical day. Even if you were 50 percent of the average daily volume, it would still take 15 days to accumulate a position of $5 million. A moderately sized hedge fund of $500 million in assets under management (AUM) would scarcely find it worth the time to concentrate on something like that, and a larger one wouldn't bother at all. However, for smaller hedge funds and for sophisticated individual investors (who are thankfully a minority in the CEF business) it can be worth taking the time to research and exploit some of the inefficiencies.

This is just one example of how small size can be a benefit. None of the opportunities in CEFs are large enough to be of any use to established hedge funds, but smaller funds can often find worthwhile trades.

## Why Size Matters

Small hedge funds have been shown to do better than the industry as a whole. There's plenty of academic research on the topic. A fairly comprehensive study was carried out by Rajesh Aggarwal from the Carlson School of Management at the University of Minnesota and Philippe Jorion from the Paul Merage School of Business at the

University of California at Irvine in 2009. It was called, "The Performance of Emerging Hedge Funds and Managers." The two authors were very thorough in taking a comprehensive database of hedge fund returns and eliminating any biases that could have overstated the results. Since hedge fund managers report their results voluntarily, it's no surprise that a newly reporting fund has just experienced strong performance. Some databases allow managers to include the previous months' returns that took place before they officially joined the database, in effect backfilling the database, so that it looks as if they've been included for longer than is the case. Aggarwal and Jorion conclude that new managers generate an additional 2.3 percent in their first two years of life, relative to later on. While this may not seem like much, the authors run statistical tests to show that it's a fairly reliable phenomenon, and compared with average annual returns of, say, 6 percent it can be a meaningful addition.

Many investors have misinterpreted historic hedge fund returns in deciding to add an alternatives allocation to their investment mix. They'll carry out a what-if analysis to see what their returns would have been like with a hedge fund allocation. They'll use an index, like HFRI, to represent hedge funds in this analysis. Most portfolios can be shown to benefit from the diversification of hedge funds when one of the popular indices (such as HFRI) is used to replicate, say, a 20 percent hedge fund allocation as part of a traditional portfolio. The results of the 1990s show more benefit than using just the last few years, but then using a longer time period is often more appropriate. However, as noted elsewhere in the book, the hedge fund industry was better when it was smaller. The diversification benefit was most pronounced when the industry was much smaller. In addition, indices such as HFRI are equally weighted rather than asset weighted, so many smaller funds are disproportionately represented. Although big funds manage most of the capital, small funds make up most of the index.

The HFRI index represents the returns of the average hedge fund, but not the portfolio of the average investor. This is a crucial difference. To use a simple example, suppose there were only two hedge funds, Jupiter and Mercury. Jupiter managed $10 billion and Mercury managed $100 million.

|            | Jupiter | Mercury | HF Index | HF Investors |
|------------|---------|---------|----------|--------------|
| **AUM**     | $10BN   | $100MM  | $10.1BN  | $10.1BN      |
| **Returns** | 6%      | 12%     | 9%       | 6.06%        |

The return of the index was 9 percent, the simple average of the two funds. But most of the money is in Jupiter and so Jupiter's returns dominate the overall returns earned by investors. If Jupiter had generated better performance than Mercury, then investors as a whole would have done better than the index. Using average returns to analyze the industry is perfectly acceptable if Jupiter is just as likely to do better than Mercury as not. But here is the crucial point: Mercury, and all the other small hedge funds out there, do on average tend to outperform big, lumbering Jupiter. Small hedge funds have outperformed big ones, and ignoring this fact has led many investors down the wrong road. The reason the average investor hasn't made money in hedge funds, while the average hedge fund has made money, is because the average hedge fund is small, and the industry itself was small when the higher returns were being generated. Investors have been marching steadily toward the mirage of yesterday's returns. As the crowd of investors seeking those returns grows, the size of the group ensures that they won't be achievable. Size has long been the enemy of hedge fund returns, and the greater the sums plowed into the industry the more assured you can be that the outcome will be disappointing.

Most of the flows into hedge funds are directed toward the larger managers, both on the basis that they are safer, but also because they have the capacity to absorb relatively large institutional allocations. This seems like a fundamental disconnect between the analysis and the implementation. Clients are basing their strategic allocation decision on one set of information, but are then implementing that allocation in a way that's critically inconsistent with their earlier analysis. They're investing in a way that doesn't reflect the history of the index on which the decision was based. Small hedge funds got them interested, but large funds are where they go.

In some respects, it's quite an amazing selective use of history. Investment products are routinely labeled with the warning that "Past performance is no guarantee of future returns." Like most warnings, it's not really helpful. It might as well be "Remember, you could lose money." Well, of course. But investors do look at past returns in analyzing hedge funds, and even though most will say they don't invest purely on the basis of historic returns, for some reason, high performance tends to attract capital. Although, in the equity and debt markets, there are "value" investors who look for unloved stocks or distressed debt and seek to take contrarian positions, I've never come across a contrarian hedge fund investor. I've met plenty of hedge fund managers who have argued that their own recent poor performance renders them an even better investment right now (and sometimes that was true) but I've never run into an investor whose strategy was to seek out distressed hedge funds. In the final analysis, investors do look at past performance in deciding where to allocate their capital and not surprisingly strong results get their attention. Hedge fund clients are, without doubt, momentum investors. They invest in what's worked in the past with the conviction that it will continue working in the future.

Nonetheless, while investors have relied on past performance of the hedge fund industry (or of the average hedge fund) to make portfolio allocations to hedge funds, they haven't taken into account the effect of industry size. In statistical terms they've assumed positive serial correlation. Serial correlation measures how likely it is that one number in a series will affect the next one. There are many examples in finance and economics—many economic statistics tend to continue in one direction for a while, before turning. Housing activity was consistently positive until 2007 and 2008, when the market crashed. New housing starts used to run at around a 1.5 million annual rate, whereas now they are around a third of that. Housing starts were serially correlated on the way up, and unfortunately on the way down. The same was true of house prices during this time. Even though hedge fund returns have been trending down, the averages have remained positive. However, there is also a relationship between size of the industry and performance. Figure 9.1 is a scatter plot that compares size with the excess return over T-bills generated by the industry each year.

Even just looking at the chart, it's clear that there's a relationship between size and returns. Returns were higher when the industry was smaller. The correlation is −0.42, showing that returns are negatively correlated with size. What's true for individual hedge funds is true for

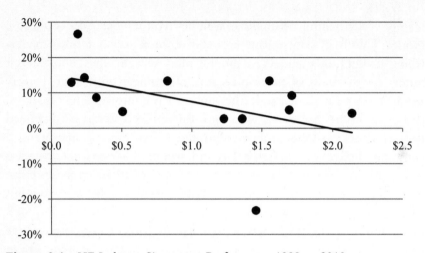

**Figure 9.1**   HF Industry Size versus Performance 1998 to 2010
Source: AUM, BarclayHedge; Returns, HFRI

the industry as a whole. Just as small hedge funds do better, so did a smaller hedge fund industry.

It's an easy mistake to make, but one that is pretty fundamental. The research on whether early stage hedge funds outperform their more established peers tends to show that they do, though some of it is inconclusive. However, the research does indicate that small, nimble, hungry managers do better. The academic paper by Aggarwal and Jorion, mentioned earlier, is probably the most thorough on the topic and their conclusion is that small is better. Nevertheless, what does seem abundantly clear is that the industry as a whole had its best years when it was small. This was no accident; it was precisely because the benefits to small size were predominant. The steady deterioration in relative returns of hedge funds, compared with traditional assets such as equities and fixed income, is surely the most compelling evidence that size hurts returns. Investors have largely been seduced, by the apparent safety of large and successful hedge funds, into thinking they can enjoy the attractive uncorrelated returns of a bygone era, while enjoying today's industrial-strength risk management, infrastructure, and reporting. It just hasn't worked. The risks have been higher overall than expected, and the returns have been lower. The blame for this must lie squarely with the investors themselves, and the advisers/consultants on whom they rely. Hedge fund managers rarely tell you why you should invest in hedge funds; they simply make the case for *their* hedge fund. Meanwhile, the consultants and funds of hedge funds have been the avid proponents of allocating to a diverse pool of managers and the consequent heavy bias toward the largest funds. And why not? If your business model is based on earning a fee on AUM, scalability is critical. Recommending lots of small investments in small hedge funds isn't a good business model, because it takes a lot more work to get the money invested.

This is where investors have allowed themselves to be badly misled. Historic industry performance reflects the average hedge fund. The average fund is small. The 80/20 rule applies to hedge funds as with so many things. The indices, particularly if you go back a few years, reflect a different composition of funds than is available today. Funds were smaller and, as a result, many strategies were available that simply don't scale with the size of today's industry. The success of the past has led to a secular change. The biggest hedge funds are large institutional asset-management companies, with all the infrastructure, processes, and research capabilities of more traditional firms. But that's not how the hedge fund industry grew. It's a consequence of its growth.

Many investors, and based on the data it might well be the majority, have failed to incorporate this into their analysis. Investing in hedge funds in the 1990s was risky back then. I know, because I was doing it. Simply finding some of the best managers relied on word of mouth referrals. There was no database that you could rely on to run a screen of funds in a particular strategy. Of course, there was little regulation and a real sense that you, the investor, were in the Wild West. These were uncharted waters, where we were discovering managers who were already highly successful, but still not widely known, because the hedge fund business itself was still so small. Back in the mid 1990s when I was helping JPMorgan find hedge funds, we often found ourselves visiting small firms with only a handful of investment staff in unassuming offices. The principals were certainly not well known to the financial media and they were operating far out of the spotlight. They weren't to be found speaking at industry conferences, and were often referred to us by some other knowledgeable investor, who was also in the hunt for unknown talent. In fact, hedge fund investing back then embraced unconventional strategies. We wanted someone with a secret sauce that while proven was not yet widely known or imitated.

A great deal of the due diligence process relied on a series of interviews with the manager trying to unlock the investment process he was using. Positions might be disclosed, but a regular data feed of daily trades was not expected. At the time, it did seem risky, but the potential returns justified it. Many talented traders had already left big firms to set up their own businesses, where they could operate with relative freedom and make some serious money.

Many of today's investors have assumed a link between yesterday's hedge fund performance and today's available managers. They take aggregate performance of the average fund, generated during a time of far less competition, and then invest in hedge funds that represent today's industry but not yesterday's. Investors want yesterday's returns without yesterday's risk. As Winston Churchill said on hearing that Britain and France had agreed to allow Germany to annex Czechoslovakia in the forlorn hope it might appease Hitler and avoid World War II, "They had to choose between war and dishonor. They chose dishonor. They will get war." Of course, the stakes are smaller. The downside is hardly global domination by an evil madman. Nevertheless, the point is that today's investors are ignoring the key features of the historic returns that have drawn them into hedge funds in the first place. They believe they can choose between having yesterday's returns with today's (more understandable) risks. To do this, they're investing in hedge funds that look nothing like those whose aggregate performance has drawn them in to this point. They're going with large, established hedge funds in order to eliminate many of the infrastructure, accounting, and operational risks a smaller, less well-financed business might face. By eliminating yesterday's risks, they're also eliminating yesterday's returns.

There's another important point that's worth making. Manager selection plays a vitally important role in an investor's results. Institutional clients routinely make strategic allocations to traditional assets such as public equities and fixed income without needing to consider whether poor individual security selection will overwhelm their returns. An investor who believes active management doesn't add value to an equity portfolio can still justify investing in equities passively, through an index fund. Earning the market return can be quite acceptable.

But for a hedge fund investor, the market return has been disappointing to say the least. The only way to successfully invest in hedge funds is to be above average at manager selection. If you can't pick managers better than the average investor, hedge funds are not a wise choice. The hedge fund industry has benefitted because most investors think they are better than average, just as most drivers do. Many hedge fund investors live in Lake Wobegon, Garrison Keillor's fictional town in Minnesota where, ". . . all the children are above average . . ."

In order to get what they want out of the hedge fund industry, investors need to take a different approach. They need to acknowledge the important role that size plays, both at the individual manager level as well as for the industry as a whole. They need to be far less comfortable investing with the crowd than is currently the case. It seems as if every day another pension fund announces that it's planning to increase its allocation to hedge funds, so as to reach the return target it's set itself to fund its obligations to retirees. It's no longer a contentious decision, and no doubt an increasing number of pension fund trustees are feeling pressure to embrace the conventional wisdom. But if it's fine to base such decisions on the historic record of the average hedge fund (which is quite respectable) then surely the historic record of the industry is an equally important consideration? If you're going to invest based on looking backward, look backward at all the information, not just selectively. Every time an institutional investor makes a decision to allocate to hedge funds, they should make clear just how they intend to confront the headwind that the industry's continued growth represents.

There is some reason to believe investors are shifting gears somewhat. Deutsche Bank released the results of a survey (reported in the *Financial Times*, March 2011) in which 65 percent of respondents expected to allocate some capital to funds with less than $1 billion in AUM, and 62 percent expected to bypass funds of hedge funds (FOHF) completely and do all their investing directly. The fees that funds of hedge funds charge on top of the hedge fund fees themselves can eat into returns, although the biggest FOHFs have substantially greater research capability than even the largest pension funds. However, the survey also found that respondents expected the industry to attract $210 billion in new inflows, which would make it challenging to direct a substantial portion to smaller managers.

## Where Will They Invest All This Money?

Many investors avoid being more than a certain percentage of a hedge funds' AUM, which limits how much they can invest with any one manager and may require a large number of different funds to accommodate their capital. Due diligence is a time-consuming business and, for this reason, strong growth in the industry is likely to continue benefitting the biggest. The Abu Dhabi Investment Authority (ADIA) is estimated to have $600 to $800 billion under management. An article in *Hedge Funds Review* by Madison Marriage in May 2011 noted that it's not worth their time to invest less than $100 million, which means if they want to remain less than 25 percent of a fund's assets, the fund itself needs to have at least $400 million.

ADIA is a notoriously demanding client as well. In my own experience at JPMorgan, just scheduling a meeting with them was a laborious process and they think nothing of changing the schedule at the last minute, or asking you to fly in from another continent at short notice. Being big can have its benefits.

Meanwhile, public pension plans continue to plow substantial sums into hedge funds. Many have overall return targets of 7 percent or higher for the assets they are managing on behalf of millions of future retirees. With interest rates in developed countries so low and returns from equities over the last 10 years disappointing, the case for adding an allocation to hedge funds as a way to meet future obligations is compelling. Preqin is a research firm that studies what these and other large investors do in the hedge fund arena. In March 2011 they released a survey covering more than 300 of the world's biggest public pension plans and similar pools of retirement savings. This group has been steadily increasing its hedge fund allocations to where they are currently 6.6 percent of total assets. They were unswayed by the 2008 crisis and related volatility, as befits a group of very long-term investors. And the returns they expect to make from hedge funds appear quite modest—around 6 percent.

However, Preqin's report goes on to note that the median pension plan surveyed has missed even this objective by more than 2 percent over the last five years, and over the last three years their returns are negative. In July 2011 the *Financial Times* reported on its own research and found that large North American pension funds were doing substantially worse with their hedge fund investments that the industry averages. (McCrum, 2011) They noted a study by academics at Yale University and Maastricht comparing the 1.9 percent earned by U.S. pension plans with the 5 percent return on the Hedge Fund Research Index from 2000 to 2008. Canadian pension plans had experienced similar results.

Moreover, even a 6 percent return may be challenging at the industry's current size. In round numbers, the hedge fund industry has $2 trillion in AUM. Risk-free rates on U.S. Treasury bonds are anywhere from 0 to 1.5 percent depending on maturity, so let's assume 1 percent is the risk-free rate. The 6 percent return assumption from hedge funds translates into a 5 percent return over the risk-free rate, or about $100 billion in annual profits on $2 trillion in AUM. The problem is, hedge funds only made this much money once in history, and that was in 2009 when they generated $200 billion. Of course that was the bounceback from 2008 when they lost almost $450 billion (based on the table of estimated profits in Chapter 4) so they lost $250 billion over two years. In order to meet the objectives of their growing client base, hedge funds need to do better than they've ever done and they need to do it every year. As more investors jump on the train before it leaves the station, their growing weight will prevent it from traveling with much speed.

If investors can incorporate some greater skepticism about what returns they can really achieve, they'll be better equipped to invest in less-travelled areas and to negotiate more attractive terms. Based on the history and the available research, it seems pretty compelling that you need to invest in small hedge funds. It's small hedge funds and a small hedge fund industry that have generated the returns. If you're going to invest based on looking back at history, invest in something that looks like the history you're looking back at. Trustees of pension funds, and others in a fiduciary role, should be far more skeptical of the consultants that show how their investment goals will be more attainable. In fact, in researching this book, I was struck by how virtually all the books on hedge funds are proponents in one form or another. For the non-finance professional, the weight of peer group pressure and positive media must make it very hard to question what is becoming conventional wisdom—namely that every institution should have an allocation to hedge funds.

Part of the problem is that the people best situated to point out some of the industry's weaknesses are making their living from it. Writing a book that terms hedge funds a mirage is not a smart career move for most people. And the closer you are to hedge funds the less reason there is to be a cynic, at least overtly.

Small hedge funds are more risky. They might be investing in less liquid stocks, have a less developed investment process, less robust infrastructure, fewer clients, and be in need of asset growth just to stay in business; but they'll also be more amenable to providing clients better terms. A large investor negotiating with a small hedge fund might obtain a separately managed account, which assures the client retains legal ownership of the assets and pretty much eliminates the risk of fraud. Even if that's not possible, the investor can demand complete daily position transparency, delivered directly from the custodian or prime broker (something we routinely did at JPMorgan, when seeding new hedge funds). The investor can probably negotiate more attractive fees, perhaps improved liquidity terms, and maybe even a stake in the business if they're one of the early investors and want to become a seed investor. All of these features play a part, both in reducing the risk of the smaller hedge fund to the investor as well as improving the potential return. Additionally, in the case of a seed investor, if the fund does turn out to be a winner, the ownership of the business can turn out to be more lucrative than the investment in the fund.

## Summary

Hedge funds will continue to attract the most talented investment managers and traders. There's nothing else that's close to providing the opportunity for serious wealth creation. If the best managers are running hedge funds, accessing the best will require being a hedge fund client. There's no other way. But investors who can recognize what made the industry so successful—and acknowledge where their goals are inconsistent with what the industry can provide—will demand better terms, transparency, liquidity, fees, and information. They'll redress the current huge imbalance that exists between the industry and its clients. By investing in hedge funds that look more like yesterday's they are likely to find the household names of tomorrow and get a fairer deal for themselves as well.

# Afterword

Having spent many years in the hedge fund industry, it's been interesting to note the reaction of my peers as they learned I was writing this book. When confronted with the central theme, that hedge fund investors would have been better off in Treasury bills, few industry insiders are shocked. In fact, I've found people respond in one of two ways. Most are unsurprised because if you work in the hedge fund industry you don't need to do the math that I've shown in this book to have an intuitive sense of how things have played out. More revealingly, a few others expressed genuine dismay that a tell-all book was being written. A cynic might conclude that this response reflected concern about highlighting past inequities and how this might upset a very comfortable business model. A more charitable conclusion is simply that nobody likes to see their industry trashed.

My hope is that this book will provoke a debate amongst investors, their advisers including funds of hedge funds, and hedge fund managers themselves. Not about the investment results though—there's no point in debating the numbers. Selecting different indices to reflect hedge fund returns or different measures of assets under management (AUM) will produce outcomes that are different but not substantively so. When I first took the time in 2010 to calculate the industry's internal rate of return (IRR) and saw my own intuition confirmed with the numerical results before me, I was amazed that nobody had done this before. Soon I came across the research paper written by Dichev and Yu (referred to in Chapter 1) which confirmed my own analysis in a thorough and robust fashion. Their results were already out in the public domain having been published in 2009, and yet few people seemed to have noticed. I found this incredible, and I contacted Ilia Dichev in 2010 to discuss his research. I thought his paper was a bombshell, a wake-up call to every hedge fund investor out there. The fact that it had received little attention probably reflected equanimity among those industry professionals who had read it. Just like the initial response of many insiders to the topic of this book, they weren't surprised; even more reason for investors to take notice.

Ilia Dichev described the overall response to his paper as "moderate". He speculated that it was because the message is "a bit of a downer". While that's probably true, I also think that since IRR is not widely used in analyzing hedge funds the enormous difference between traditionally calculated results based on average annual returns and the asset-weighted results that reflect how investors have really done are not readily apparent. Although few hedge fund professionals have expressed surprise to me at these results, most outside the industry are quite taken aback. I've discussed this with people who have a reasonably sophisticated knowledge of investing but are not directly involved in hedge funds, and like most of us they assume fabulously wealthy hedge fund managers are the result of similarly successful clients. This illustrates a huge misconception in popular opinion, and highlights the need for some changes. If this book serves as a catalyst for needed debate, it will have more than served its purpose.

The questions the industry should ask itself include:

- Why have overall results for clients been so poor?
- What is an appropriate fee model that is fair for clients but appropriately rewards high-decile investment performance?
- What rights over transparency, liquidity, and governance should investors demand for their hedge fund investments?
- Are these results likely to persist in the future?

These issues are worth examining, because it's not as if hedge funds haven't made money. They just haven't passed those profits back to their investors. There's no shortage of immense investment talent available, although there's almost certainly too much capital in hedge funds today for the available opportunity set.

As with so many products in finance, part of the problem is that there's no obvious business model to profit from a negative view (after all, it's not easy to short hedge funds). There's an entire industry, including hedge funds of funds, prime brokers, consultants, and others whose central purpose is to channel assets to hedge funds. And economies of scale dictate at every step that the larger funds will be favored. There's little demand for consultants or advisers who profess skepticism, and no doubt those individuals who do simply make their careers elsewhere.

This book began as an essay in *AR* published in November 2010 (Hedge fund IRR has been pathetic). While the title was more biting than I might have chosen, it did draw attention and subsequent discussions convinced me I had a story that hadn't yet been told. I started out believing the villains were the hedge fund managers and all the advisers who had channelled substantially too much capital to them. But my view shifted as I researched the book, and if there is a fault it lies squarely with many supposedly sophisticated investors who have applied far less critical analysis and cynicism to their allocation decisions. An industry has developed to meet demand, and the buyers have freely agreed to pay high prices for often mediocre results.

Saying hedge funds have been a bad investment for many should not be confused with saying they're all bad, or that nobody has made money. There are many supremely talented hedge fund managers who have provided enormous value to their astute clients, and there are many highly successful clients of hedge funds. That will most likely always be the case. I know numerous people who are extremely happy with their investments. A hedge fund is the most lucrative asset-management business around and will continue to draw the very best talent. Some investors will always beat the averages, and demonstrate an ability to select high-decile managers before their returns deteriorate. But winning investors and value-providing hedge funds are not typical of the whole industry, and it's doubtful that will change at anything like its current size.

The importance of manager selection was noted in Chapter 9. Since earning the average return on a hedge fund portfolio hasn't beaten Treasury bills it's safe to say that picking the right managers is indispensable for success. Average manager selection ability renders a hedge fund portfolio pointless. This should play well to allocators and consultants, since an important element of their value proposition is that they are good at picking tomorrow's winners. Of course many of them are, but it's worth noting just how difficult that is, and not just because we can't all be above average.

Using the BarclayHedge database of hedge fund returns and AUM provides some measure of the challenge. Their database covers around a third of the industry by AUM, so it represents a fairly good sample. It includes more than 3,300 funds in total for whatever period of time they've reported, including many that have closed down. Like all hedge fund databases it suffers from the fact that managers report voluntarily, creating the survivor bias shortcoming in that poorly performing funds are generally not included and so returns in total are somewhat over-stated. Analyzing the results beginning in 1994, if an investor could select funds that were at the sixtieth percentile or higher (i.e., better than 60 percent of all funds) he would have gained an additional 3.7 percent in annual performance compared with the asset-weighted average. This could be enough to make his hedge fund portfolio worth-while. Only 40 percent of the industry by AUM is typically this good in any one year, but that's still a sizeable selection to choose from.

However, the difficulty in selecting funds at the sixtieth percentile or higher is illustrated by the fact that funds routinely move in and out of the top tier of performance. In other words, there is limited persis-tence in good performance. Across the entire database for example, I found that for funds that were at the sixtieth percentile or better for any one year, they spent half of their existence below this level. On this basis a good fund may only be good every other year. Very few funds are consistently top performers. In fact, only 7 percent of the funds that were ever better than the sixtieth percentile managed to repeat that performance for every year of their lives. Far more common is for a relatively good year to be followed by a relatively poor year, and so on.

But hedge funds are not stocks. If your strategy is to buy the worst performing names in the S&P 500 every year and sell the best performers, it's not very complicated to execute. Trading in and out of hedge funds annually is pretty much implausible. The due diligence is time consuming, redemption terms far less than the liquidity available in publicly traded equities, and many hedge fund managers would shun clients who tried to time their investments in this way. Hedge fund investments are intended to be held for years, and the infrequency of consistently strong performance makes it that much harder for any portfolio to contain mostly winners year after year.

At the time of writing (August 2011) the year is shaping up to be another challenging one for the industry. While this may appear to be driven by events outside anyone's control (such as falling global equities), the central assertions of this book are that past performance for investors has been poor, and that future results will be no different without changes that include reducing the size of the industry. Since 2002, hedge funds have failed every year to beat a simple blend of 60 percent equities/40 percent high-grade bonds. Annual returns have slipped while AUM has risen, and at its current size hedge funds need to generate record trading profits every year to meet the fairly modest return expectations of their institutional client bases. This looks like a long shot. I look forward to watching events unfold.

# Bibliography

Adamson, L. "Factoring in the Unknown." *Absolute Return*, October 24, 2008. Retrieved September 20, 2011. http://www.absolutereturn-alpha.com/Article/2035705/Factoring-in-the-Unknown.html.

Aggarwal, R.K. and Jorion, P. "Hidden Survivorship in Hedge Fund Returns." *Financial Analysts Journal*, 66, no. 2 (2010). Retrieved September 20, 2011. http://www.cfapubs.org/doi/pdf/10.2469/faj.v66.n2.1.

Avery, H. "AI Market Roundup—Hedge Fund Fees Come Down." *Euromoney*, November 2008. Retrieved September 20, 2011. http://www.euromoney.com/Article/2039075/BackIssue/65744/AI-market-round-up-Hedge-fund-fees-come-down.html.

"Bernard Madoff Overview." *New York Times*, Updated August 23, 2011. Retrieved June 23, 2011. http://topics.nytimes.com/top/reference/timestopics/people/m/bernard_l_madoff/index.html?scp=1-spot&sq=madoff&st=cse.

Bowman, L. "Hands Up: Who Wants to Call the Bottom of the Market." *Euromoney*, December 2008. Retrieved September 20, 2011. http://www. euromoney.com/Article/2060571/Hands-up-who-wants-to-call-the-bottom-of -the-market.html.

Boyd, R. "Lehman Collapse Puts Hedge Fund in Dire Straights. *Fortune*, October 10, 2008. Retrieved September 20, 2011. http://money.cnn.com/2008/10/10/ news/economy/river_boyd.fortune/index.htm.

Boyson, N. "Hedge Fund Performance Persistence: A New Approach." *Financial Analysts Journal*, 64, no. 6 (2008). Retrieved September 20, 2011. http:// www.northeastern.edu/nicoleboyson/persistence.pdf.

Rothfeld, M. and Bray, C. "Madoff Trustee Targets Fairfield." *Wall Street Journal*, July 22, 2010. Retrieved September 20, 2011. http://online.wsj.com/article/ SB10001424052748704684604575381024250819284.html.

Brewster, D. "Money Flows out of Hedge Funds at Record Rate." *Financial Times*, December 31, 2008. Retrieved September 20, 2011. http:// www.ft.com/intl/cms/s/0/8bdfc056-d6db-11dd-9bf7-000077b07658 .html#axzz1YWEnMGqo.

Denmark, R. "Investors at the Gate." *Absolute Return*, March 27, 2008. Retrieved September 20, 2011. http://www.absolutereturn-alpha.com/Article/1897113/ Investors-at-the-Gate.html.

Dichev, I.D. and Yu, G. "Higher risk, lower returns: What hedge fund investors really earn." *Journal of Financial Economics*, August 4, 2010. Retrieved October 2010. http://www.people.hbs.edu/gyu/HigherRiskLowerReturns.pdf.

"Fine print in Hedge Fund Charters Makes it Hard to Oust Poorly Performing Directors. *Alpha Magazine*, February 24, 2009. Retrieved September 20, 2011. http://www.absolutereturn-alpha.com/Article/2113458/Search/Mutiny -Good-Luck.html?Keywords=Fine+print+in+Hedge+Fund+Charters+Makes +it+Hard+to+Oust+Poorly+Performing+Directors.+Alpha+Magazine.

Hall, C. "From Manhattan to Madoff: The Causes and Lessons of Hedge Fund Operational Failure" *Castle Hall Alternatives*, August 19, 2009. Retrieved June 23, 2011. http://www.castlehallalternatives.com/upload/publications/ 2507_ManhattantoMadoffPaper.pdf.

Johnson, S. "Hedge Funds Driving Stock Collapse." *Financial Times*, October 13, 2008. Retrieved March, 2011. http://www.ft.com/intl/cms/s/0/623d939a -98ce-11dd-ace3-000077b07658.html#axzz1YGLX4PbU.

Jones, S. "Investors Seek Transparency in Hedge Funds." *Financial Times*, November 9, 2010. http://www.ft.com/intl/cms/s/0/ee29d874-eb5f-11df -b482-00144feab49a.html#axzz1YGLX4PbU.

Kaulessar, R. "Hedge Fund to Pay Back NFL Owner's Investment." *HedgeFund. net*, August 9, 2011. http://www.hedgefund.net/publicnews/default.aspx ?story=12775.

Lewis, M. *The Big Short*. New York: Norton & Co, 2011.

Lowenstein, R. *When Genius Failed*. New York: Random House, 2000.

Mackintosh, J. "Hard Hit Hedge Funds Forced to Renegotiate Banking Terms." *Financial Times*, December 5, 2008. Retrieved August 2011. http://www.ft.com/intl/cms/s/0/16c27a02-c26d-11dd-a350-000077b07658.html#axzz1YWXgoWXY.

—. "Hedge Fund Withdrawal Expected by Managers." *Financial Times*, September 30, 2008. Retrieved August 2011. http://www.ft.com/intl/cms/s/0/ad490a5a-8e87-11dd-9b46-0000779fd18c.html#axzz1YWXgoWXY.

—. "Hedge Funds Extend Redemption Ban." *Financial Times*, November 29, 2008. http://www.ft.com/intl/cms/s/0/583ea4e4-bd84-11dd-bba1-0000779fd18c.html#axzz1YGLX4PbU.

—. "Record 40bn is Redeemed From Poorly Performing Hedge Funds." *Financial Times*, November 21, 2008. Retrieved August 2011. http://www.ft.com/intl/cms/s/0/f8012178-b76c-11dd-8e01-0000779fd18c.html#axzz1YWXgoWXY.

—. "Top 10 Hedge Funds Make $28bn." *Financial Times*, March 1, 2011. Retrieved August 2011. http://www.ft.com/intl/cms/s/0/24193cbe-4433-11e0-931d-00144feab49a.html#axzz1YWXgoWXY.

Mallaby, S. *More Money Than God*. New York: The Penguin Press, 2010.

Markopolos, H. *No One Would Listen: A True Financial Thriller*. Hoboken: John Wiley& Sons, 2011.

McGeehan, P. "The Markets: Market Place; Chase Manhattan Must Cut Its Revenue After Discovering Some Nonexistent Trading Profits." *New York Times* November 2, 1999. Retrieved September 20, 2011. http://www.nytimes.com/1999/11/02/business/markets-market-place-chase-manhattan-must-cut-its-revenue-after-discovering-some.html?scp=1&sq=goggins&st=nyt.

Singer, P. "Elliot Changes Fees; Investors Shrug." *Absolute Return*, December 18, 2009. Retrieved August 2011. http://www.absolutereturn-alpha.com/Article/2361653/Elliott-changes-fees-investors-shrug.html.

Paulson, Jr., H.M. *On the Brink: Inside the Race to Stop the Collapse of the Global Financial System*. New York: Hachette Book Group, 2010.

Pool, B. & Bollen, N. "Do Hedge Fund Managers Misreport Returns? Evidence from the Pooled Distribution." *American Finance Association*, (2007). Retrieved January 2011. http://www.afajof.org/afa/forthcoming/5706.pdf.

Rose-Smith, I. "Goodbye, Easy Money." *Institutional Investor*, October 24, 2008. Retrieved September 21, 2011. http://www.institutionalinvestor.com/Article/2035698/Good-Bye-Easy-Money.html?ArticleId=2035698.

SEC. "SEC Litigation Release 19631." March 30, 2006. Retrieved March 2011. http://www.sec.gov/litigation/litreleases/lr19631.htm

Sender, H. "Hedge Funds Exploiting Rivals' Woes." *Financial Times*, October 3, 2008. Retrieved March 2011. http://www.ft.com/intl/cms/s/0/63840190 -90e4-11dd-8abb-0000779fd18c.html#axzz1YWXgoWXY.

—. "Why Hedge Funds are Clinging to Investors' Cash." *Financial Times*, December 13, 2008. Retrieved March 2011. http://www.ft.com/intl/cms/s/0/ 66ef9630-c8b8-11dd-b86f-000077b07658.html#axzz1YWEnMGqo.

Slater, R. *Soros: The World's Most Influential Investor*. New York: McGraw Hill, 2009.

Sorkin, A. R. "Princeton Endowment Posts a 14.7% Return." *New York Times*, October 15, 2010. Retrieved September 21, 2011. http://www.nytimes .com/2010/10/16/business/16princeton.html.

Sorkin, A. *Too Big to Fail*. New York: Penguin Group, 2010.

Taub, S. "The New Hedge Fund Economics." *Absolute Return*, October 24, 2008. Retrieved September 21, 2011. http://www.absolutereturn-alpha.com/ Article/2035736/New-Hedge-Fund-Economics.html.

Vardi, N. "The Vanishing Hedge Fund." *Forbes Magazine*, September 16, 2009. Retrieved September 21, 2011. http://www.forbes.com/forbes/2009/1005/ companies-stagg-capital-vanishing-hedge-fund.html.

Williamson, C. "Liquidity Hunt Hits Managers." *Pensions & Investments*, November 10, 2008. Retrieved March 2011. http://www.pionline.com/article/ 20081110/PRINTSUB/311109937.

—. "Redemption Requests Bode Ill." *Pensions & Investments*, December 8, 2008. Retrieved March 2011. http://www.pionline.com/article/20081208/ PRINTSUB/312089980/1031/TOC.

Zuckerman, G. *The Greatest Trade Ever*. New York: Broadway Books, 2009.

# About the Author

S imon Lack spent 23 years with JPMorgan before retiring to manage his own money in 2009. Much of his career with JPMorgan was spent in North American Fixed Income Derivatives and Forward FX trading, a business that he ran successfully through several bank mergers and numerous economic cycles.

He sat on JPMorgan's investment committee, allocating more than $1 billion to hedge fund managers and founded the JPMorgan Incubator Funds, two private-equity vehicles that took economic stakes in emerging hedge fund managers.

Simon now runs SL Advisors, LLC, an investment firm he founded in 2009, where he manages money for himself and clients in a variety of strategies. Simon serves on the Board of Trustees of

Wardlaw-Hartridge School in Edison, New Jersey, where he chairs the Investment Committee, and also chairs the Memorial Endowment Trust Investment Committee of St. Paul's Church in Westfield, New Jersey. Simon is a CFA Charterholder. He grew up in the United Kingdom and moved to the United States in 1982. He lives in Westfield, New Jersey, with his wife and three children.

# Index